Council Ta

Step By Step Guide On How To Lose The Fear Of The M [illegible]
Bullying By The Local Authorities Financial Departmen [illegible] Residents
Who Fall In to Arrears.

PAUL PATTERSON

ISBN: 9798320058153

CONTENTS

INTRODUCTION

Those of you who have ever fallen in arrears with council tax will be well aware of the councils' procedure.

Reminder notice.

Firstly you will receive a reminder notice, which will state you need to bring your account up to date within 7 days. If payment is not received as requested on the reminder notice, recovery action may continue and a summons issued.

If you make payment of the sum requested on the reminder notice, no further action is taken as long as you continue to make payment of your remaining monthly instalments on time.

Final notice.

The council will only issue two reminder notices to you during one financial year.

If you are late paying for a third time in a year, you will be issued with a final notice, which will cancel your monthly instalments.

Your instalment plan will only be reinstated if you bring your instalments up to date and set up a direct debit to ensure future payments are made on time.

If payment is not received as requested on the final notice, recovery action will continue and a summons issued.

So, you can find yourself being summonsed to the magistrates' court for owing as little as one month of arrears.

What people are not aware of is that councils all over the country are acting unlawful, they are highly inflating their costs in summonsing people to court. Councils can only charge for reasonable costs 'incurred.'

Everyone who receives a council tax summons needs to attend their hearing, in doing so this will create chaos and panic for councils and magistrates.

JUSTICES' CLERKS' SOCIETY
2011
Revised 2023

Procedure in Liability Order Applications

1. Background

Council has been contacted by Peter Downton of HMCS Enforcement Team concerning the way HMCS records the making of liability orders in Council Tax cases, due to challenges to the process in various quarters, including questions from MPs.

The concerns raised are:

a) that the procedure is not transparent;

b) HMCS can not demonstrate that it is accurately recording the orders made.

c) whether the orders are in correct form since they are not wet-ink signed.

Council has considered the issues, and in light of the procedures operating in their courts is of the view that the following process is lawful and transparent.

The key objective of any procedure is that an accurate record is made of every decision of the court and retained. It is not possible for each individual complaint to be case entered, recorded, and resulted, (save by a massive expansion in the number of legal advisers and court assistants). However the objective is achieved within existing resources by recording results against the council's printout and retaining that as an annexe to the register.

For legal guidance in dealing with council tax enforcement, see JCS's Council Tax Guide on the civil page of the JCS pages in the Intranet.

2. Procedure: issuing summons

1. The council delivers one or two complaint lists to the court with their fee (or an undertaking to pay it later)

2. The list is reviewed by a legal adviser or other member of staff with delegated powers who issues or refuses to issue the summonses.

3. Where the complaint list was sent by email (which will be normal), the legal adviser forwards the email back to the court office (forwarding ensures the complaint list is attached to the email) stating their decision. The court office then emails with council with the result and files the legal adviser's email with the attached complaint list.

4. Where the complaint list is sent in hard copy, either one copy of the list is returned endorsed to the council and the court retains the other endorsed list, or the court retains a single endorsed list and the council is informed of the result.

5. Whether the process is digital or by hard copy, the decision must be recorded and retained for three years under the Retention and Destruction Policy.

6. The council then prints and serves the summonses.

7. The Magistrates' Courts Rules do not require a signature on summonses, however a council's software may affix one. If the name is wrong (e.g. it refers to a justices' clerk), that is a defect of form, and is not fatal to the summons or the subsequent proceedings (Magistrates' Courts Act s. 123).

3. Procedure: Liability Order application

1. Since 2021, this procedure may be carried out by audio or video link. Parties should always be permitted to appear in person if they wish however.

2. The legal adviser is given an up to date printout of the Council's applications by a Council representative. This will set out the name and details of each defendant and against that the order the Council wishes the court to make.

3. The court hears a bulk application for all non-attenders: the Council representative proves the technical requirements on oath and gives evidence that the sums levied have not been paid.

4. Any defendant attending or writing to the court is dealt with individually and orders made (or not made) in their case. Their attendance or otherwise is also recorded.

5. The legal adviser records the overall number of liability orders made, withdrawn, dismissed and adjourned. This may be recorded on a file cover or on the copy printout, or both.

6. In addition for each case where the court does not make the order set out in the Council's printout, the legal adviser notes the actual order made against the defendant's name in the printout.

7. This means that there is a definitive record on the Council's printout of all orders made.

8. The numbers of orders granted, withdrawn etc. recorded by the legal adviser, are input after court and appear in the Libra register.

9. Any adjourned cases are individually case-entered and resulted (to generate a door list and appearance in the Libra diary).

10. The council's printout, marked up by the legal adviser, is kept permanently, as an annexe to the court register. The results are disclosable under Rules 66ff MCR 1981 (there is a certified extract template onto which the result should be copied).

4. Orders

The order is made when the presiding justice pronounces it, and is recorded in the court register, see section 3. Since repeal of the prescribed order, there has been no court produced order. The Council's software should generate a notice that the order has been made, which is sent to the defendant. They should not be signed or endorsed with the name of a JP or court officer (still less a justices' clerk!)

Some councils are still sending out their notification in the form of a liability order, but even so it is not a court-generated document, it is notification of the order made by the justices.

5. Procedures prior to the hearing

The Court and its staff should not give the impression that the Council is in charge of the process.

If a respondent writes asking for an adjournment the court should ask the Council for its views, but the decision on an adjournment should be made by a bench, or by a member of staff with powers to adjourn. Under no circumstances should the correspondence simply be sent to the Council, or respondents told to deal directly with the council in relation to adjournments.

If respondents wish to enter into negotiations with the council about payment they should be directed to the Council, but advised that the court hearing will remain fixed until further notice.

6. Appearance

It is normal and good practice for respondents to be referred to the Council's staff when they attend court. Many cases are settled effectively at that stage, saving court and Council time, and reducing the strain on the respondent. Ushers and receptionists should therefore advise respondents of this service.

Nonetheless this is not a legal requirement, and court staff should not insist that respondents must see a Council representative, or refuse to call their case on until they have. If respondents want their 10 minutes in court, they have a right to them. A defendant who has to be pressurised into speaking to the Council is not likely to make an effective arrangement in any event.

THE DAY THE SUMMONS ARRIVES

Once the summons arrives you need to take notice of the date it was delivered, as the court have to give 14 clear days prior to the hearing date. Councils send out summonses 1st class post and summonses are classed as being serviced two days after posting.

Now is the time to challenge the councils costs which they have added to the summon, they can only lawfully add costs reasonably incurred up to gaining the liability order. Councils unlawfully add costs which were not reasonably incurred in gaining the liability order. You also need to challenge the lawfulness of the summons. Many councils pre date the summons before the court legal adviser has heard the complaint. The council expect to receive approval to print and issue summonses on the same day they lay the complaint by email. On many occasions the court office are too busy to reply the same day, and a few days can pass before the council get approval to print and issue the summonses. So on many occasions the local authorities are failing to give those summonsed 14 full clear days notice of their hearing.

You now email your challenge to the court and the council in one email.

Template For Challenging Costs and Lawfulness of Summons.

Name
Address
Post Code

22nd January 2024

FAO
Swansea Magistrates' Court
Clerk to the Justices
Neath Port Talbot County Borough Council Legal Team

Re: Case No: 24888 / Account Reference: 660973796 Hearing date 13/02/2024

Re: Challenge to the councils tax summons costs

Re: Challenge to the lawfulness of the summons

Dear Swansea Magistrates' Court & Neath Port Talbot County Borough Council,

I have been summonsed to a council tax hearing sitting at Swansea Magistrates Court on13/02/ 2024

1. I will be challenging the councils costs. For me to challenge the councils costs, can you please:

Send me copies of a 'detailed' breakdown of costs and calculation which have already been approved by the magistrates for council tax summonses for:

2022-2023

2023-2024

2. I will be challenging the lawfulness of the summons. For me to challenge the lawfulness of the summons, can you please:

Send me copies of the original complaint made to the clerk to the justices, with all names except my name redacted. I also request a copy of the email trail which shows that this list was sent to the Court and the summonses were authorised by a legal adviser.

Confirm that I am removed from the council's 'bulk order' so that the court can deal with my matter individually; as I shall be asking for an adjournment, until these important issues can be addressed.

Yours faithfully,

Name.

Example of a reply.

On 13 Feb 2024, at 10:35, Revenues <Revenues@rushcliffe.gov.uk> wrote:

□

OFFICIAL

Mrs Xxxx Xxxxxxx | Council Tax account number xxx44876
The Lodge Station Road xxxxxxx xxxxxxxx xxxxxx

Dear Xxxx Xxxxxxx

Further to your email below. I have attached the documents / copies of emails as requested. Your account remains unpaid with the enforcement agent.

Yours sincerely

David Sills
Revenues Team Leader
Rushcliffe Borough Council

Reply to Mr Sills.

13th February 2024

Rushcliffe Borough
CouncilRevenues Team
Leader

Re: Account No: xxx44876

Dear David Sills,

Thank you for your letter by email 10.35am 13th February 2024

Well David, we are entering Alice in Wonderland territory, 'Sentence first, verdict afterwards'

The complaint **<u>must come first</u>**, followed by the issue of a summons.

My summons was invalid on the face of it through non-compliance.

I was issued a summons with many others in a bulk listing with a summons stating issuedate 29th November 2023. This summons was issued before the court legal advisor approved the bulk listing complaint on 4th December 2023

The impression given is that it is in fact the council which is in charge of the council tax hearings.

JUSTICES' CLERKS' SOCIETY
Procedure in Liability Order Applications
Dated: April 2011

5. Procedures prior to the hearing

The Court and it's staff should not give the impression that the council is in charge of the process.

JUSTICES' CLERKS' SOCIETY
Procedure in Liability Order Applications
Dated: April 2011

1. Procedure: issuing summons

The council deliver one or more complaint lists to the court with their fee (or an understanding to pay it later)

The list is reviewed by a legal adviser with delegated powers who issues the summons. Either one copy of the list is returned to the council and the court retains the other endorsed list, or the court retains a single endorsed list and the council is informed of the outcome (in reality it is extremely unlikely that any summonses will not be issued sothis does not need to be a detailed notification). The council then print the summonses,

I think it is time to bring this to the attention of my MP and MoJ who it has beensuggested referring to, given there is a Parliamentary precedent from 2009.

Council tax enforcement in magistrates' courts

Bridget Prentice made this statement concerning council tax enforcement inmagistrates' courts.

The Parliamentary Under-Secretary of State, Ministry of Justice (Bridget Prentice):

'Local authorities use the magistrates' courts to enforce non-payment of council tax. This process begins with an application (called a 'complaint') for the court to issue a summons informing the individual that the local authority is seeking unpaid council tax and asking theindividual to attend court if they wish to challenge the court making a liability order for that amount. The issue of a summons for non-payment of council tax or non-domestic rates must be authorised by a Justice of the Peace or Legal Adviser with delegated powers froma Justices' Clerk. Fees are chargeable and the decision of the court at the hearing must berecorded in a court register.

Investigations by Her Majesty's Courts Service (HMCS) staff have identified examples of asmall number of magistrates' courts failing to follow the correct procedures. In particular HMCS has identified examples of fees not being charged to local authorities for issuing proceedings and some examples of a failure at Salford magistrates' court to enter the results of applications for liability orders on the court register. More seriously two
magistrates' courts, Rochdale and Salford permitted the local authorities to issue summonses requiring attendance at court without the authorisation of the court.

This was a clear procedural failing and was immediately stopped when it came to light. Individuals and the magistrates concerned in subsequently hearing cases would not have been aware of this irregularity.

In all such cases individuals would have had ample opportunity to attend court if they wished to challenge the liability to have the non-payment enforced against them. However,they would not have been aware that the summons had not been properly issued. Had thesummonses been correctly issued, there is no reason to think the consequences wouldhave been any different in practice. Individuals should pay their council tax and this Housewould expect non-payment to be properly enforced.

Given the paucity of information available it is not practicable to identify the individuals concerned. The issues identified in Rochdale and Salford have been fully investigated andI am satisfied that correct procedures are now in place. A national check was carried out that revealed no similar practices and all courts have been reminded of the importance of following the correct procedures.'

You state, 'Your account remains unpaid with the enforcement agent.'

On the condition that all summons costs and enforcement agents removed. I will considermaking a direct arrangement to pay £20.00 per month off arrears, considering I will shortlybe receiving a demand for 2024-25.

Yours faithfully,

,

On 14 Feb 2024, at 09:48, Revenues <Revenues@rushcliffe.gov.uk> wrote:

OFFICIAL

Good Morning

Re:Council Tax account number 40544865
The Lodge xxxxxx xxxxx xxxxxxx xxxxxxxxxxxxxx xxxx

Thank you for your letter attached to this email.

The complaint list was provided to the Nottingham Magistrates Court on 29 November 2023. It was signed and returned and summons were then produced and sent out.

The correct procedures have been followed and the liability order is valid.
Please contact the Enforcement Agents Penham Excel Ltd to arrange payment.

Kind Regards
Julie Viliunas
Revenues Officer
Rushcliffe Borough Council

REPLY

18th February 2024

Nottingham Magistrates
Court Legal Advisers

Rushcliffe Borough
CouncilRevenues Officer

Re: Account No: xxx44876

Dear Julie Viliunas,

Thank you for your letter by email 9.45am 14th February 2024

You state that the correct procedures have been followed and the liability order is valid.
It seems that the correct procedure was not followed, as the authority to print and issue the summons was not given to the council until 4th December 2023 by the court legal adviser for the hearing on 18th December 2023. The council failed to give me14 clear days notice of the hearing.

For council tax there must be at least 14 clear days

It seems I have remedy by way of application for the summons to be dismissed by the magistrates court, or by way of judicial review application no later than 18th March 2024.

Yours faithfully,

Xxxx Xxxxxxx

COUNCILS REPLY

OFFICIAL

Dear Xxxx Xxxxxxx

Thank you for your email of the 14 February 2024 and your comments are noted.

I would confirm that I have withdrawn your account from the enforcement agent. I have removed the liability order and summons from your account along with the associated costs.

I note we have since received a direct debit mandate from you. I have arranged for your payment facility to be updated. A copy Council Tax demand is attached and a hard copy is being issued by post.

May I take this opportunity to apologise for any undue stress or inconvenience this matter may have caused.

David Sills
Revenues Team Leader
Rushcliffe Borough Council

Challenging Costs

St Albans Magistrates are acting unlawful in allowing Dacorum Borough Council to claim:
Post Enforcement Collection (After granting of the Liability Order.) £329,945.52

The council can only claim costs reasonably 'incurred' up to gaining the liability order and no further.

High Court Case ruling of: CO/976/2014

Justice Andrews stated in the approved judgement:

35. It is clear that there must be a sufficient link between the costs in question and the process of obtaining the liability order. It would obviously be impermissible (for example) to include in the costs claimed any element referable to the costs of executing the order after it was obtain, or to the overall administration of council tax in the area concerned.

To challenge the councils costs you have to go through the breakdown of figures they will send you, searching for costs they have not reasonably incurred in gaining the liability order. If they do not send you a breakdown of costs before the hearing you should ask for an adjournment as you can not challenge their costs without this breakdown.

My previous book 'The Great Council Tax Recovery Scam' goes into detail on how to challenge costs.

Copy of the breakdown of costs and calculation which have been approved by the magistrates for council tax summonses for Dacorum Borough Council

IRRV Narrative based Version

Name of Authority DacorumBoroughCouncil
Enforcement Costs Formula based on Gross Costs of Collection for Council Tax & Business Rates

Cost of administration from general ledger	1,099,898.40	
Revenues Billing 30%	329,969.52	
Enforcement (summons to hearing) 30%	329,969.52	**A**
Enforcement (hearing) 10%	109,989.84	**B**
Post enforcement collection (after grant of liability order) 30%	329,969.52	
Total	1,099,898.40	
Number of accounts with summons issued	4,700	**C**
Number of accounts with liability order granted	3,600	**D**
Admin cost per summons (A/C)	70.21	**E**
Admin cost per liability order (B/D)	30.55	**F**
Total admin cost for account with liability order (E+F)	100.76	

Where a liability order has been made:

The Council Tax (Administration and Enforcement) Regulations 1992

Duties of debtors subject to liability order

36.—(1) Where a liability order has been made, the debtor against whom it was made shall, during such time as the amount in respect of which the order was made remains wholly or partly unpaid, be under a duty to supply relevant information to the billing authority on whose application it was made.

(2) For the purposes of paragraph (1), relevant information is such information as fulfils the following conditions—

(b) the billing authority requests him by notice given in writing to supply it; and

(c) it falls within paragraph (3).

(3) Information falls within this paragraph if it is specifed in the notice mentioned in paragraph (2)(b) and it falls within one or more of the following descriptions—

(a) information as to the name and address of an employer of the debtor;

(b) information as to earnings or expected earnings of the debtor;

(c) information as to deductions and expected deductions from such earnings in respect of the matters referred to in paragraphs (a) to (c) of the definition of "net earnings" in regulation 32 or attachment of earnings orders made under this Part, the Attachment of Earnings Act 1971(1) or the Child Support Act 1991(2);

(d) information as to the debtor's work or identity number in an employment, or such other information as will enable an employer of the debtor to identify him;

(e) information as to sources of income of the debtor other than an employer of his;

(f) information as to whether another person is jointly and severally liable with the debtor for the whole or any part of the amount in respect of which the order was made.

(4) Information is to be supplied within 14 days of the day on which the request is made.

Unless you are in real financial hardship I would not advise you to give any of the above information, as the council are mainly only interested in identifying who your employer is, so they can then put an Attachment of Earnings order on your wages. This order is not a court order, it is a council order.

The Council Tax (Administration and Enforcement) Regulations 1992

SCHEDULE 4 DEDUCTIONS TO BE MADE UNDER ATTACHMENT OF EARNINGS ORDER

TABLE A

DEDUCTIONS FROM WEEKLY EARNINGS

(1)	*(2)*
Net earnings	*Deduction rate %*
Not exceeding £35	0
Exceeding £35 but not exceeding £65	3
Exceeding £65 but not exceeding £90	5
Exceeding £90 but not exceeding £110	7
Exceeding £110 but not exceeding £175	12
Exceeding £175 but not exceeding £250	17
Exceeding £250	17 in respect of the first £250 and 50 in respect of the remainder

TABLE B

DEDUCTIONS FROM MONTHLY EARNINGS

(1)	*(2)*
Net earnings	*Deduction rate %*
Not exceeding £152	0
Exceeding £152 but not exceeding £260	3
Exceeding £260 but not exceeding £360	5
Exceeding £360 but not exceeding £440	7
Exceeding £440 but not exceeding £700	12
Exceeding £700 but not exceeding	17

(1)	*(2)*
Net earnings	*Deduction rate %*
£1,000	
Exceeding £1,000	17 in respect of the first £1,000 and 50 in respect of the remainder

TABLE C

DEDUCTIONS FROM DAILY EARNINGS

(1)	*(2)*
Net earnings	*Deduction rate %*
Not exceeding £5	0
Exceeding £5 but not exceeding £9	3
Exceeding £9 but not exceeding £13	5
Exceeding £13 but not exceeding £16	7
Exceeding £16 but not exceeding £25	12
Exceeding £25 but not exceeding £36	17
Exceeding £36	17 in respect of the first £36 and 50 in respect of the remainder

If you are struggling to survive with an Attachment of Earnings Order on your wages, you can attempt to have the order removed by emailing or writing to the CEO of the council with the following template:

Template downloadable at:

https://docs.google.com/document/d/18-IfEArXytBuW8D_zW2sq36NRgvQg1cl/edit?usp=sharing&ouid=111889191575252819642&rtpof=true&sd=true

Name
Address Line 2
Address Line 3
Post Code

Name of CEO
Name & Address of council

Council Tax Account Number ########

Dear Name of CEO,

I currently have an Attachment to my earnings, to pay off my council tax arrears for account number ######, the amount being taken out of my pay to cover the attachment is putting me and my family into financial difficulty whereby I am finding it difficult to pay other household bills, typically my rent/mortgage and utility bills.

The plight I am in is in direct contravention to Article 11 of the International Covenant of Economic, Social and Cultural Rights,which was ratified by the UK government in 1976 which states:-

ARTICLE 11

" The States Parties to the present Covenant recognize the right of everyone to an adequate standard of living for himself and his family, including adequate food, clothing and housing, and to the continuous improvement of living conditions. The States Parties will take appropriate steps to ensure the realization of this right, recognizing to this effect the essential importance of international co-operation based on free consent. "

Also the amount being taken out of my pay is in contravention to Article 7 A Subsection 2 of the International Covenant of Economic,Social and Cultural Rights which states :-

ARTICLE 7

The States Parties to the present Covenant recognize the right of everyone to the enjoyment of just and favourable conditions of work which ensure, in particular:

(a) Remuneration which provides all workers, as a minimum, with:

(ii) A decent living for themselves and their families in accordance with the provisions of the present Covenant.

I point you to Paragraph 72 of The Limburg Principles on the Implementation of the International Covenant on Economic, Social and Cultural Rights,which sets out violations of the above covenant,in particular, A State party will be in violation of the Covenant, inter alia, if: it wilfully fails to meet a generally accepted international minimum standard of achievement, which is within its powers to meet;

Taking this into account, I would ask that you as CEO of my council suspend the AOE,

So as I may come to a suitable arrangement to pay off my council tax with affordable payments, so my Human Rights are not violated.
I would also like to this opportunity to apply for a section 13 A reduction as per the Local Government Finance Act 1992 which states,:-

LOCAL GOVERNMENT FINANCE ACT 1992 SECTION 13 A

"Where a person is liable to pay council tax in respect of any chargeable dwelling and any day, the billing authority for the area in which the dwelling is situated may reduce the amount which he is liable to pay as respects the dwelling and the day to such extent as it thinks fit."

To bring my council tax to a more affordable level,whereby I can live with human dignity as per the human rights act.

I look forward to your reply.

Yours faithfully

Your Name.

Some councils do reduce or remove these attachment of earnings order when challenged.

Below is a reply to the above template:

Dear Mr Xxxxx

Thank you for your email.

The amount deducted from your wages is deducted at a percentage rate which is laid down in the regulations and some employer's payroll systems are hardcoded to deduct these amounts.

However, we are happy for you to contact your employer's payroll office and ask them to reduce the amount that is being taken – as long as it isn't reduced to a very small amount. You can also ask your payroll section to call us for clarification that we are ok with this.

Please also go to our website re the S13A as there is an online application form on there.

Regards

Revenue Team

Yvette Deaney

Revenues & Benefits Administrator.

If you are struggling and can show financial hardship you can put in a section 13a application to have your arrears reduced or zeroed. You should apply for council tax support before applying for a s13a.

Section 13A template

Name
Address

Post Code

Date 10/02/2024

Wokingham Borough Council
Council Tax Recovery Section

Formal Request under Section 13 to reduce or write off council tax liability
Re: Council Tax xxxxxxxx

To Recovery Officer,

I write to make this formal request to the council to consider using its discretionary power under Section 13 (a) of the Local Government Finance Act 1992 to discharge my council tax liability obligation which is outstanding due to a variety of justifiable and conscionable reasons.

This request is made because, it is clear that the liability is in all probability never going to be paid. The amount demanded is liable to force me to live on an income below the government poverty threshold (The UK government, the European Union and many other countries use 60 percent of median household income as the poverty 'threshold').

I accept it, is the authority's discretion alone to exercise this privilege under the above-mentioned law, but I make this request to you in writing as my very last resort to resolve this issue and it is my utmost hope that we can come to this arrangement mutually and agreeable to all concerned.

I really need help, (put all your problems here).........................

I trust I shall hear from you in regards to this matter at your earliest convenience,
]
Yours faithfully,

Name.

Distress.

45.—(1)Where a liability order has been made, the authority which applied for the order may levy the appropriate amount by distress and sale of the goods of the debtor against whom the order was made.

(2) The appropriate amount for the purposes of paragraph (1) is the aggregate of—

(a) an amount equal to any outstanding sum which is or forms part of the amount in respect of which the liability order was made, and

(b) a sum determined in accordance with Schedule 5 in respect of charges connected with the distress.

(3) If, before any goods are seized, the appropriate amount (including charges arising up to the time of the payment or tender) is paid or tendered to the authority, the authority shall accept the amount and the levy shall not be proceeded with.

(4) Where an authority has seized goods of the debtor in pursuance of the distress, but before sale of those goods the appropriate amount (including charges arising up to the time of the payment or tender) is paid or tendered to the authority, the authority shall accept the amount, the sale shall not be proceeded with and the goods shall be made available for collection by the debtor.

(5) The person levying distress on behalf of an authority **shall carry with him the written authorisation of the authority, which he shall show to the debtor if so requested;** and he shall hand to the debtor or leave at the premises where the distress is levied a copy of this regulation and Schedule 5 and a memorandum setting out the appropriate amount, and shall hand to the debtor a copy of any close or walking possession agreement entered into.

(6) A distress may be made anywhere in England and Wales.

(7) A distress shall not be deemed unlawful on account of any defect or want of form in the liability order, and no person making a distress shall be deemed a trespasser on that account; and no person making a distress shall be deemed a trespasser from the

beginning on account of any subsequent irregularity in making the distress, but a person sustaining special damage by reason of the subsequent irregularity may recover full satisfaction for the special damage (and no more) by proceedings in trespass or otherwise.

(8) The provisions of this regulation shall not affect the operation of any enactment which protects goods of any class from distress.

(9) Nothing in the Distress (Costs) Act 1817(1), as extended by the Distress (Costs) Act 1827(2), (which makes provision as to the costs and expenses of the levying of certain distresses) shall apply to a distress under this regulation.

Remember the enforcement agent must not breach both Tribunals, Courts and Enforcement Act 2007 Schedule 12 paragraph 26 and Section 45.—(5) of The Council Tax (Administration and Enforcement) Regulations 1992

Tribunals, Courts and Enforcement Act 2007 SCHEDULE 12

26 (1)

The enforcement agent must on request show the debtor and any person who appears to him to be in charge of the premises evidence of—

(a) his identity, and

(b) his authority to enter the premises.

(2) The request may be made before the enforcement agent enters the premises or while he is there.

45.—(5) of **The Council Tax (Administration and Enforcement) Regulations 1992** States, The person levying distress on behalf of an authority **'shall carry with him the written authorisation of the authority, which he shall show to the debtor if so requested;'**

NOTICE FROM THE BAILIFFS (ENFORCEMENT AGENTS)

'Your belongings will e removed unless you pay the total amount you owe' is always in bold print on the enforcement agents recovery notice. These notices are designed to put fear in you. Never allow them to intimidate you. They can not force entry, they can only enter through open or unlocked doors.

Section 45.—(5) of **The Council Tax (Administration and Enforcement) Regulations 1992** States, The person levying distress on behalf of an authority **'shall carry with him the written authorisation of the authority, which he shall show to the debtor if so requested;'...**

The suggestion that the council can authorise enforcement agents to enter premises and take control of goods is problematic, it is an unfortunate piece of drafting, it can not form the basis for authority for the enforcement agents to enter premises for council tax.

Not only do they have to show their written authority pursuant to Regulation 45 of The Council Tax (Administration and Enforcement) regulation 1992 but they have to show their judicial authority pursuant to paragraph 26(1) of Schedule 12 of The Tribunals, Courts and Enforcement Act 2007

The liability order does not exist in paper form.

So, soon as you receive an enforcement agency notice, you need to send by email the following template to that agency.

Name
Address
Post code

19th March 2024

Jacobs Enforcement Agents

Jacobs Ref:xx3xxxxx

Council tax Ref: xxxxxxxxxx

Dear Jacobs,

Before any of your agents step foot onto my property I request a copy of your judicial authority to enter my property.

Breach paragraph 26 of **Tribunals, Courts and Enforcement Act 2007 SCHEDULE 12 and** paragraph 66 of schedule 12 will provide me with remedy in damages**.**

Any visit without giving sight of any 'court authority' with our name on will lead to court action, as in the case of **Leighton v Bristow Sutor 20th SEPTEMBER 2023(AS APPROVED)**

Please do not reply with:

1. We are not obliged to supply a copy of the Liability Orders nor do our Certificated Enforcement Agents need to carry it with them to legitimise their powers.'

2. Every enforcement agent will carry a Letter of Authority from the client in question, along with their identification and their Certification from the Court.'

To this His Hon Judge Harrison stated, 'It is, in my judgment, difficult to conclude that the defendants had a reasonable belief that they were acting in accordance withthe Schedule, when the basis for doing so seemed originally to have been a letter from their client, purporting to give authority.'

3. Should you wish to verify the legitimacy of our involvement or obtain a copy of the Liability Orders in question, you will need to contact the Council directly.'

To this His Judge Harrison states, 'In my judgment, a householder is entitled to ask the defendants on what authority they are purporting to enter his property, and the

fact that they cannot do so, and refer him back, effectively to their client, is almost bound to cause him to be dissatisfied. **Inmy judgment, the defendants are in breach of paragraph 26.**

It seems you at Jacobs are so confused with the Leighton V Bristow Sutor Case Law.

You not only have to comply with, The Council Tax (Administration and Enforcement) Regulations 1992

Distress. 45- (5) The person levying distress on behalf of an authority **shall carry with him the written authorisation of the authority, which he shall show to the debtor if so requested;**

Which Judge Harrison stated does not give the authority for an enforcement agent to enter onto a property, but also you have to comply to:

Tribunals, Courts and Enforcement Act 2007 SCHEDULE 12
26 (1)
The enforcement agent must on request show the debtor and any person who appears to him to be in charge of the premises evidence of—
(b) his authority to enter the premises.
(2) The request may be made before the enforcement agent enters the premises or while he is there.

Judge Harrison stated that, 'The suggestion that the council, can authorise enforcement agents to enter premises and take control of goods is problematic, it is an unfortunate piece of drafting, it can not form the basis for authority for the enforcement agents to enter premises for council tax.'

Not only do you have to show your written authority pursuant to Regulation 45 of The Council Tax (Administration and Enforcement) Regulations 1992 but you have to show your judicial authority pursuant to paragraph 26(1) of Schedule 12 of The Tribunals, Courts and Enforcement Act 2007

The liability 'order' does not exist in paper form, it only exists in the hands of the council as a liability 'notice.'

JUSTICES' CLERKS' SOCIETY
2011
Revised 2023Procedure in Liability Order Applications
4. Orders
The order is made when the presiding justice pronounces it, and is recorded in the court register, see section 3. Since repeal of the prescribed order, there has been no court produced order. The Council's software should generate a notice that the order has been

made, which is sent to the defendant. They should not be signed or endorsed with the name of a JP or court officer (still less a justices' clerk!)

Some councils are still sending out their notification in the form of a liability order, but even so it is not a court-generated document, it is notification of the order made by the justices.

Once again I inform you that if one of your enforcement agents visits my property without the full judicial authority, as stated by Judge Harrison, I will take the same action as Wayne Leighton took against Bristow & Sutor.

No further notice will be given to you.

Yours faithfully,

Name.

The Taking Control of Goods Regulations 2013

Exempt goods

4.—(1) Subject to paragraph (2) and to regulation 5, the following goods of the debtor are exempt goods—

(a) items or equipment (for example, tools, books, telephones, computer equipment and vehicles) which are necessary for use personally by the debtor in the debtor's employment, business, trade, profession, study or education, except that in any case the aggregate value of the items or equipment to which this exemption is applied shall not exceed £1,350;

(b) such clothing, bedding, furniture, household equipment, items and provisions as are reasonably required to satisfy the basic domestic needs of the debtor and every member of the debtor's household, including (but not restricted to)—

(i) a cooker or microwave;

(ii) a refrigerator;

(iii) a washing machine;

(iv) a dining table large enough, and sufficient dining chairs, to seat the debtor and every member of the debtor's household;

(v) beds and bedding sufficient for the debtor and every member of the debtor's household;

(vi) one landline telephone, or if there is no landline telephone at the premises, a mobile or internet telephone which may be used by the debtor or a member of the debtor's household;

(vii) any item or equipment reasonably required for—

(aa) the medical care of the debtor or any member of the debtor's household;

(bb) safety in the dwelling-house; or

(cc) an older person;

(c) assistance dogs (including guide dogs, hearing dogs and dogs for disabled persons), sheep dogs, guard dogs or domestic pets;

(d) a vehicle on which a valid disabled person's badge is displayed because it is used for, or in relation to which there are reasonable grounds for believing that it is used for, the carriage of a disabled person;

(e) a vehicle (whether in public ownership or not) which is being used for, or in relation to which there are reasonable grounds for believing that it is used for, police, fire or ambulance purposes; and
(f) a vehicle displaying a valid British Medical Association badge or other health emergency badge because it is being used for, or in relation to which there are reasonable grounds for believing that it is used for, health emergency purposes.
Link to The Taking Control of Goods Regulations 2013
https://www.legislation.gov.uk/uksi/2013/1894/contents/made

Ref. J90SA002

IN THE HIGH COURT OF JUSTICE
KING'S BENCH DIVISION SWANSEA
DISTRICT REGISTRY

Before HIS HONOUR JUDGE HARRISON (Sitting as a Judge of the High Court)

IN THE MATTER OF

WAYNE LEIGHTON (Claimant)

-v-

BRISTOW AND SUTOR (Defendant)

THE CLAIMANT appeared in person
MR C FENDER appeared on behalf of the Defendant

JUDGMENT
20th SEPTEMBER 2023 (AS APPROVED)

JUDGE HARRISON:

This case concerns claims made by Mr Wayne Leighton regarding the activity of the defendants, who are an enforcement agency based in Worcestershire, but who carry out enforcement work for local authorities on a national basis. The agency were instructed by City of York Council to pursue council tax liabilities said to be owed by

Mr Leighton in relation to 2 Oldman Court in York. This property was owned by the claimant but not occupied by him; rather, it was let under a tenancy agreement and/or was unoccupied.

The agency contends that they were instructed to enforce four liability orders obtained by the council over the period 2015 and 2021, and acted accordingly. The claimant argues that in fact, in seeking to enforce the same, the defendant acted unlawfully in a number of ways, or a number of different alternative ways, for which liability in damages attaches. These can be summarised as follows:

> Breach or paragraph 66 of the Tribunals and Courts Enforcement Act 2007,the TCEA
> Harassment, contrary to section 3 of the Protection from Harassment Act1997
> Breach of the Statute of Marlborough 1267, and
> Breach of a commercial lien.

Mr Leighton has represented himself in these proceedings. It is clear that these are mattersabout which he feels strongly, and in respect of which he has invested much time and research. It is equally clear that much of his concern is directed towards the City of York Council, who are not party to these proceedings.

Background

In order to understand these proceedings, it is perhaps necessary to consider briefly thebackground. Mr Leighton was aggrieved at how the City of York Council dealt with his council tax liability. Specifically, he considered that he should have had some discount fromhis liabilities over the relevant years for periods when Oldman Court was unoccupied. It appears that the City of York Council had, in the exercise of its discretion, made a decision not to apply discounts to vacant properties. Mr Leighton wanted to challenge this, and sought disclosure of documentation relevant to the decision-making process. He felt, indeed he feels, that he did not get a satisfactory response, and informed the council of his intention to challenge their decision. He also felt that in relation to at least some of the periods of council tax claimed, the liability was that of his tenant, rather than his own.

Notwithstanding this, the council proceeded to enforce what they saw as a legitimate obligation on the claimant, and one which they felt they were obliged to pursue. The procedure for enforcement involved issuing a summons to appear before the Magistrates' Court. It is worth noting in passing that this area of enforcement is one of those areas that remains within the remit of the Magistrates' Court, albeit perhaps, for reasons that may become apparent within this judgment, it is one which is ripe for reform.

Mr Leighton only answered one of the summonses. That was the first, and it was the summons sent to his address at number 175 Kingsway West in York.

Thereafter and in relation to subsequent years, summons were sent to 2 Oldman Court. During this period, the claimant was out of the country, travelling, and he says he was unaware of the same. Oldman Court was let under a tenancy agreement for at least part of the relevant periods. The liability order purported to be enforced by the defendants arose from these summons.

During the course of this case, I received evidence from Mr Paul Sanderson, the revenues and benefits manager at the City of York Council. He explained the process by which liability orders were obtained by the City of York. Specifically, he explained how liability orders were granted by the Magistrates. In many ways, the term "order" is a misnomer, if used in the same way as might be understood in the civil courts of Wales and England. No physical individual order as such is ever actually produced by the court. Rather, the presenting officer on behalf of the council attends, with a list of those summons to appear. Having heard anyone who does attend the court, and subject to any amendment, the list is simply signed by a magistrate, and the liability order is deemed to be made.

Mr Leighton makes a number of points about this process, and challenges its legitimacy. He points to the apparent tension between what ordinarily is thought of as a valid order of the court, and that which this process produces. By way of example, he contends that this is not a proper record of the proceedings. It does not identify clearly the maker of the order, and it is neither stamped, nor sealed. Further, insofar as it purports to be the basis for an award of costs, then it does not comply with the obligation to make clear whether or in what sum such costs are rewarded. Of equal importance in these proceedings, Mr Leighton makes the point that, in the absence of any paper record, then the court should not be satisfied that any such liability order was ever made against him.

There is, of course, an important practical point to Mr Leighton's complaints about the order. This particular method by which liability orders are produced means that there is no record retained by the court regarding making the same. How then, Mr Leighton asks, is he, as a subject of such an order, able to apply to set such an order aside and/or appeal the same? He says that is precisely what he wanted to do in this case, but when he tried to do so, his attempts revealed the flaw in the process, and potentially Article 6 of the European Convention on Human Rights is engaged.

Before moving on from the process before the Magistrates' Court, Mr Leighton also invites me to reflect upon the issue of service. The documents in this case reveal that, save for the first summons, all of the other summons were served on 2 Oldman Court. Mr Leighton points to the fact that at this time he had told the council that he was not resident at that address. In fact, that was the whole point of his argument. Nevertheless, he argues they presumably went to the court and pursued it in his absence, when service of the summons could not be established.

In completing my brief synopsis of the background to this claim, it is necessary to note the following: in passing the claim to the enforcement agents, the council simply send a list of persons against whom liability orders have been obtained. The defendants, on the evidence, taken them at their word and proceed accordingly. In their defence, drafted on 15 June of 2022, they plead that they have a general authority to proceed with enforcement from the council. This document is signed by Mr Sanderson, as the corporate income manager of City of York Council, it is dated 18 April 2014, and appears at page 65 of the trial bundle. Itreads as follows:

> "In accordance with the Tribunals, Courts and Enforcement Act 2007, we authorise enforcement agents employed by Bristow and Sutor to enter premises and take control of goods, in connection with debts owed to the City of York Council."

As the case has progressed before me, Mr Fender, counsel for the defendant, recognised thatthis document could not be read as providing authority to the defendant to do what the letter says. Rather, it can only amount to a written confirmation of instructions to the defendants toact on behalf of the council.

<u>The relevant law and analysis</u>

<u>Tribunals and Courts Enforcement Act 2007</u>

The nature of the work upon which the defendants were engaged is strictly regulated. In this case, it is Schedule 12 of the Tribunal and Courts Enforcement Act 2007 that is most relevant to my considerations. Paragraph 66 of Schedule 12 provides:

> "Remedies available to the debtor
>
> This paragraph applies when an enforcement agent -
>
> > breaches a provision of the Schedule, or
> > acts under an enforcement power under a writ, warrant, liability order or other instrument that is defective.
>
> That breach or defect does not make the enforcement agent of a person he is acting for a trespasser.

But the debtor may bring proceedings under this paragraph.

…

(5) In the proceedings the court may -

(a) order the goods to be returned to the debtor,

(b) order the enforcement agent or any related party to pay damages in respect of loss suffered by the debtor as a result of the breach, or of anything done under the defective instrument."

Sub-paragraph (6), sub-paragraph (7), I move onto sub-paragraph (8):

"(8) Sub-paragraph (5)(b) does not apply where the enforcement agent acted in the reasonable belief -

(a) that he was not breaching a provision of the Schedule, or

(b) (as the case may be) that the instrument was not defective"

Mr Leighton advances his case under paragraph 66 in two ways: firstly, he argues that the defendants have proceeded under a defective instrument, in that no liability orders were in fact made in his case, and/or if they were made, then they should not have been made, for the reasons that I have attempted to outline above, by way of background.

The first point that I have to consider is whether I am satisfied that liability orders were actually made by the magistrates. The practice of obtaining a liability order as set out above is potentially problematic for a local authority, or, indeed, any enforcement agent trying to prove that it was made. Here the documents provided to the court appeared at trial bundle 247 to 255, repeated as better copies at trial bundle 273 to 279, comprise effectively extracts from court lists, showing that on the material day the claimant was on the court list, and pairing that with a signature applied at the end of the list by a magistrate or district judge.

The documents, as I say, do reveal a series of problems with the process. By way of an example, the name of the individual making the order is not readily discernible. Secondly, what the magistrate or judges certify is the number of liability orders made that day. For example, by way of what appears at trial bundle page 277, the magistrates certify that on 21 June 2017, 1,474 liability orders were made.
The defendants argue that, when that document is read in conjunction with the extract of the court list, at trial bundle page 276, then that is enough to establish that Mr Leighton was one of the 1,474. However, the way in which the orders are made certainly makes it difficult for an absent debtor either to challenge the same by applying to set aside, or even appeal the same. In fact, that which appears at trial bundle page 277 goes further than the documents provided in relation to different dates, in that the document at page 277 records an amount of costs to be applied. The other similar documents do not make such a recording. This discrepancy is surprising, to say the least.

However, putting my misgivings about the process aside, it seems to me that it is necessary to remind myself that City of York Council are not the defendants in this case. If I ask myself, on the balance of probabilities, whether the Magistrates' Court on the dates shown made liability orders against those persons on the court list, then the contemporaneous documentation suggests that this was the case. Insofar as Mr Leighton gave evidence that his recollection was that no order was made on the one occasion that he attended the Magistrates' Court, then in that regard he must be mistaken; I prefer the evidence set out in the documents.

Whether Article 6 of the Convention on Human Rights is engaged, or whether or not the form of the order is capable of challenge is not, in my judgment, central to the resolution that I must resolve in this case. What is relevant is that I am satisfied, on the balance of probabilities, that the Magistrates' Court indicated they were granting liability orders against those shown in the list on the days in question. Furthermore, the council noted the making of the same, and the council then passed on that information to the defendants for enforcement.

Putting oneself in the defendants' position, they were being told by a public body that, for enforcement purposes, liability orders had been obtained against individuals on a list. For the purposes of paragraph 66(8)(b), that would amount for grounds for a reasonable belief on the part of the enforcement agent that there was in existence a non-defective instrument. It was not, in my judgment, necessary, in order for the enforcement agent to have a reasonable belief, for him to go further and enquire how the order was obtained, or the process involved.

Whilst I am persuaded that paragraph 66(8)(b) is an answer to an argument regarding any defect in the instrument itself, I would reiterate my concerns that the process does, in myjudgment, cause the problems that I set out in the following paragraphs.

The second point made by the claimant regarding the defendants' failings relates to the argument that in any event there has been a breach of the Schedule. Specifically, he alleges that paragraph 26 is engaged. That paragraph provides as follows:

> "(1) The enforcement agent must on request show the debtorand any person who appears to him to be in charge of the premises evidence of -
>
> his identity, and his authority to enter the premises.
>
> (2) The request can be made before the enforcement officerenters the premises, or while he is there."

The claimant says that in the context of this case, he has requested provision of the defendants' authority and it was not provided. Specifically, he points to the refusal of the defendants to provide a copy of the liability order on request, or otherwise to identify underwhat authority they were intending to enter his premises. For example, reference can be made to trial bundle page 96.

The defendant argues that these provisions should be read as being restricted to the time of the actual visit itself. In other words, paragraph 26 is restricted to requests made as the enforcement agent enters the premises, or whilst there. Here they say Mr Leighton was never present when agents visited, and so no request relevant to this paragraph could be made. Whilst tenants were there on occasions, and whilst agents did visit Mr Leighton's parents at 28 Elvington Park, neither of those, it is submitted, requested sight of authority toenter.

In his skeleton argument, Mr Fender, for the defendant, argues that the authority for an enforcement agent to act comes from the enforcement provisions as set out in paragraph 7 ofSchedule 12. Paragraph 7 provides:

> "(1) An enforcement agent may not take control of goods unlessthe debtor has been given notice.
>
> (2) Regulations must state -
>
> (a) the minimum period of notice,

(b) the form of the notice,

(c) how it must be given,

(d) who must give it.

The enforcement agent must keep a record of the time when the notice has been given.

(3) If regulations authorise it, the court may order in prescribed circumstances that the notice given may be less than the minimum period.

(4) The order may be subject to conditions."

Not unreasonably, Mr Leighton points to that section of the amended defence to which I have already referred above. Paragraph 11 of the amended defence, trial bundle page 45, specifically reads as follows: "With regards to paragraph 4 and 5 of the particulars, the authority of an enforcement officer to enter a premises is given by the council. A copy of one of the letters of authority is attached hereto, marked BS2. Pursuant to paragraph 26(1)(b)of Schedule 12 of the Tribunal, Courts and Enforcements Act 2007, a copy of the relevant authority is carried by the enforcement agent, so that it can be provided if it is asked for by any party upon the agent attending the premises."

Now, as set out above, Mr Fender, for the defendants, recognises the problem with this document. The suggestion that the council, as effectively clients, can authorise employees ofthe defendant to enter premises and take control of goods is problematic, to say the least. Mr Fender characterises the document as an unfortunate piece of drafting, and concedes it could not form the basis for authority for the defendant to enter premises. Hence his argument that the authority for the defendants comes from paragraph 7.

There are, in my view, a number of problems with this assertion. Firstly, paragraph 7 is not drafted in a way to confer authority. Rather, it restricts what an agent can do. Secondly, it is in contradiction with the specifically pleaded paragraph that I have set out above. Whilst I do not regard this as fatal to Mr Fender's argument, the point can properly be made that the pleading must have been made on clear instructions from the defendants as to how they regarded this document. Thirdly, paragraph 18(xi) of the amended defence, bundle 49, is even more specific. It reads:

"On 14 June 2016, the defendant emailed the claimant in response to an email received on 13 June 2016. The

> defendant explained that there was no requirement for their office of the enforcement agent to hold a copy of the liability order, as the defendant is acting as agent for the council, and as referenced inparagraph 7 above. The defendant hold that there is a different between the liability order obtained by the council and letter of authority the defendant holds to enter the premises to take control of goods, which is what is required by paragraph 26(1)(b) of Schedule 12 of the Tribunal, Courts and Enforcement Act 2007. While the defendant may not hold copy of the liability orders, they still held the relevant authority from the council to enforce their orders."

Lastly, and perhaps most obviously, Sarah Brown for the defendant gave evidence to the court to the effect that the defendants regarded the council's document as being the relevant authority, and furthermore, as the pleadings say, the document was carried by the agents when attending to enforce council tax liabilities, and was presumably produced by agents for that purpose. It follows that the defendants did not themselves regard paragraph 7 as providing authority to them to act, and even if it was, it rather begs the question of what they would show to a householder if they were asked to produce it.

In any event, Mr Fender argues that there is no breach of Schedule 12 paragraph 26, because no request was made contemporaneously to the attendance of the agent at the relevant premises. He submits that this paragraph should be construed as being restricted tothe occasion when the agent is physically at the premises. Whilst I can see why this would be the usual situation, I cannot read the paragraph as being so restrictive. If a householder knows that an agent will visit, why should he not seek sight of any authority in advance? There is no doubt that Mr Leighton made it clear that he wanted to see the defendants' authority to enter his premises, and whilst he may himself have focused on having sight of liability orders, it is not, in my judgment, sufficient simply to signpost him to the local authority. In this case, and for the reasons explained above, we have no physical, individual order that can be shown by the defendants to the claimant. He is simply told to contact the local authority. In my judgment, a householder is entitled to ask the defendants on what authority they are purporting to enter his property, and the fact that they cannot do so, and refer him back, effectively to their client, is almost bound to cause him to be dissatisfied. In my judgment, the defendants are in breach of paragraph 26.

It is perhaps illuminating to note that, according to the defendants' own evidence, if a request had been made on the day of a visit, then the likelihood is that the householder would have been shown a document that the defendants now accept did not amount to the relevant authority. Furthermore in this respect, I am unable to conclude that the defendant can escape responsibility by relying upon paragraph 66(8)(b). It is, in my judgment, difficult to conclude that the defendants had a reasonable belief that they were acting in accordance with the Schedule, when the basis for doing so seemed originally to have been a letter from their client, purporting to give authority. The provisions at paragraph 26 require the defendant to be able to put themselves in a position where they can provide on request their authority to act. That, it seems to me, is an important obligation placed upon them, and is something in respect of which they needed to address their minds, and make arrangements accordingly. Otherwise they run the risk of not being able to tell the claimant anything useful, and simply signposting him to a client, which is what they have purported to do here.

Protection from Harassment Act 1997

> "A person must not pursue a course of conduct -
>
> which amounts to harassment of another, and
>
> which he knows or ought to know amounts to harassment of the other."

Section 7 of the Act provides as follows:

> "(2) References to harassing a person must include alarming theperson or causing the person distress."

"A course of conduct" is defined as follows:

> "It must involve -
>
> (a)in the case of conduct in relation to a single person, conducton at least two occasions in relation to that person, or
>
> (b)in the case of conduct in relation to two or more persons,conduct on at least one occasion in relation to each of those persons."

Thus to succeed, a claimant must establish (1) a course of conduct, (2) that course of conductmust amount to harassment, and (3) the defendant must know or ought to have known that the course of conduct amounted to harassment.

The assessment of the alleged conduct is by way of an objective test. It is the point of view of the alleged victim of harassment that is relevant to this objective test, and the test canbe met by correspondence. See *Ferguson v British Gas Trading Limited* [2009]

EWCA 46. In *Dowson & Ors v Chief Constable of Northumbria* [2010] EWHC 2612, Simon J provided some assistance in the consideration of what was required:

> "(a) There must be conduct which occurs on at least twooccasions,
>
> (b) which is targeted at the claimant,
>
> (c) which is calculated in an objective sense to alarm or distress,
>
> (d) which is objectively judged to be oppressive and unacceptable,
>
> (e) what is oppressive and unacceptable may depend on the social or working context in which the conduct occurs, and
>
> (f) a line has to be drawn between conduct which is unattractiveand unreasonable, and conduct which has been described in various ways as torment of the victim, or is of an order which would sustain criminal liability."

Section 1(3) of the 1997 Act sets out statutory defences to the Act as follows - I summarise:

> "Subsection (1) or (1A) does not apply to a course of conduct ifthe person who pursued it"

- the relevant sub-paragraphs being (b) and (c) -

> "(b) that it was pursued under any enactment or rule of law, orto comply with any condition or requirement imposed by any person under any enactment, or
>
> (c) that in the particular circumstances, the pursuit of the courseof conduct was reasonable."The argument advanced by Mr Leighton as regards this element of the claim is reasonably straightforward. He contends that during the period complained of, there were a total of about 35

enforcement actions by the defendants in various forms of contact, including email and correspondence. There were 15 visits to three separate properties, namely Kingsway West, Oldman Court and Elvington Park. Whilst the claimant was not present for any of the visits, his tenants were present at Oldman Court some of the time, and his parents were at Elvington Park for the two visits made in April and June 2021. The defendants do not contend otherwise, and at paragraph 11 of the amended defence, set out the Schedule of the 15 visits.

Mr Leighton points to the upset caused by the prospect of visits of this sort. He also points to the type of correspondence received by way of enforcement visit warning, for example, at trial bundle 302, warning the recipient that his goods were banned, that there would be a return visit, and that costs could become substantial. Mr Leighton explained that the visits to the premises occupied by his parents were particularly troublesome for him. He felt that the defendants were using them as a means to get to him.

Set against this, the defendants argue that on any proper analysis of the evidence, their activity could not be categorised as actionable harassment. In order to make a proper assessment of the same, they submit that the court must first look at the period over which the activity is alleged. Here the relevant period is between May 2015 and June 2021, a period a little over six years. Mr Fender submitted, and it was not contradicted, that within that period there were periods of no enforcement activity taking place at all. On his calculations, made at paragraph 20 of the skeleton argument, there were a total of about four and a half years out of the six during which no activity took place. If, it is submitted, this is combined with the fact that the defendants were dealing with four separate liability orders, then the amount of contact is consistent with fairly normal enforcement activity.

Of course the court cannot ignore the fact that the work undertaken by the defendants by definition involves sending letters and undertaking visits to people who would rather not receive the same. While such contact might still amount to harassment in the right circumstances, it does seem to me that the court has to approach the same with a degree of care when applying the guidance set out in *Dowson.* Can the conduct be said to be objectively oppressive and unacceptable when considered against the working context in which it occurs? Is the conduct over the period alleged such that the court can conclude that the threshold for a finding of harassment is met - ie, the conduct is of an order that would sustain criminal liability if proved to the requisite standard?

In my judgment, the conduct does not reach that threshold, especially seen in the context of enforcement activity. In my judgment, the period over which the activity tookplace and the long periods of no activity lead me to that conclusion.

The statute of Marlborough 1267

The claimant raises this ancient provision as potentially giving rise for a cause of action for him against the defendants. Specifically, he contends that the Act prohibits unreasonable distresses wherein it provides:

> "None from henceforth shall cause any distress that he hath taken to be driven out of the county where it is was taken, and ifone neighbour do so to another, of its own authority and without judgment, he shall make fine, as above is said, as for a thing done against the peace. Nevertheless, if the Lord presume so to do against his tenant, he shall be grievously punished by amerciament. Moreover, distresses shall be reasonable and not too great, and he that taketh great and unreasonable distresses shall be grievously amerced for the excess of such distresses."

Now, apart from the fact that the language is far removed from today, it is of course relevant to try to analyse what the statute was intended to prevent. The practice of exercising distresses over another person's property or livestock involves taking control or impounding the same. The Statute of Marlborough is intended to limit the practice of distress to that which is reasonable. The Act provides a penalty, by way of amerciament, to be applied to any person taking unreasonable distress. What is an amerciament? In *Dayani v Bromley LBC* [1999] 3 EGLR 1 44, the court considered a different part of the 1267 statute, and was referred to the meaning of amerciament provided in Jowitt's Dictionary of English Law. The definition is set out in that judgment. Whilst the court appears not to have ruled decisively on the issue, the following is relevant to my consideration. Namely, an amerciament was a punishment for an offence, and was described as being "more merciful than a fine". They were, it is said, a source of revenue to the Crown.

In my view, therefore, the statute was not intended to convey a right of action for damages on an individual. Rather, as submitted by Mr Fender for the defendants, it takes its place as part of the criminal law, whereby an individual could be fined or amerced for a transgression. It is also difficult to see what the provisions of the statute would add to the claimant's case in this particular action.

The commercial lien

Whilst travelling in Thailand in 2015, Mr Leighton appears to have visited a notary, to draw up a notice. The document is dated and signed by Mr Leighton before the notary on 13August 2015, and appears at trial bundle 337. It was sent on to the defendants' email address. In that document Mr Leighton states as follows:

> "Your unlawful, nonsensical, threatening correspondence has caused me to suffer a tort. Any future unlawful correspondencefrom your corporation will be the subject of a commercial lien in the sum of £10,000 sterling. All agents, representatives and individuals should be made aware that they are subject under common law for full commercial liability for their actions, and inform any bonding agents or insurers accordingly. Any furthercontact from you or anyone acting on behalf of your corporation will be confirmation of this contract."

Mr Leighton contends that, rather like a motorist driving into a car park might be deemed to accept the terms and conditions of the same regarding parking his vehicle, so the defendants, in continuing in this case with their conduct of contacting him and visiting his property, should be held liable to accepting a contractual liability of £10,000.

Applying first principles of contract, it cannot, in my judgment, be said that the defendants accepted the terms as set out in that document. There was no meeting of the minds of the claimant and the defendants on this issue, and it simply cannot be inferred that the defendants accepted that in attending the property, for example, they accepted a contractual liability to the claimant in the way now alleged. The defendants were not seeking to attend the property pursuant to the alleged contractual term; rather, they attended pursuant to their work as enforcement agents. Whilst, as considered above, their conduct in this regardis rightly regulated, the claimant cannot, in my judgment, unilaterally impose such conditions, as he appears to have tried to do.

Conclusion

In summary, I am satisfied that the claimant has established a breach of paragraph 26 ofthe Schedule, in that the defendants failed to provide evidence of their authority. I am not persuaded that the other pleaded causes of action are established. For reasons that I have set out above, there is a danger in conflating Mr Leighton's grievance with the City of York Council with the position of the defendants. Mr Leighton's Article 6 argument is a case in point. Whilst I have made such observations as I am able about the process adopted to obtain liability orders, I remind myself that City of York Council are not party to the proceedings, and therefore have not had the opportunity to argue their position in detail. I have confined myself to the position of the defendants, who, as enforcement agents, are rightly subject to the regulatory framework of the 2007 Act.

Having established such a breach, paragraph 66 provides the claimant will remedy in damages. There is no real guidance as to how the same should be assessed. Here there is no obvious, direct pecuniary loss. The claimant has, however, suffered a non-pecuniary loss by way of injury to feelings and/or frustration, consequent upon the protracted period of engagement between the claimant and the defendants on this issue. The claimant invested significant time in this matter, and was plainly frustrated by what he saw as the defendants' failure to appreciate what he was asking for, together with their persistence in continuing with a process against a background of what I have concluded was a breach of the Schedule on their part.

In my judgment, the quantum of any award would not be the same as for an harassment case, albeit, the approach adopted by the courts in such cases is informative. Harassment cases themselves have often turned to discrimination cases for guidance. Specifically, the approach in the *Chief Constable of West Yorkshire Police v Vento (No 2)* [2003] ICR 318. The court is also mindful of the view expressed by Nicol J in *S & D Property Investments Limited v Nisbet* [2009] EWHC 1726 (Ch). Here the point was made that discrimination, by its very nature, involved an element of humiliation for being treated differently, and this is generally absent from most harassment claims.

In reaching a conclusion as to this non-pecuniary loss, it is relevant to consider the period over which the conduct complained of persisted, and it is relevant to consider that effectively the conduct is one of a repeated breach, perhaps caused by a lack of understanding of their obligations under the Schedule. Whilst the defendants might have been somewhat dismissive of the claimant's point, I am not satisfied that they behaved in a way that suggested either malice or bad faith on their part. We now know that they felt that the letter from City of York Council was enough to act. As it transpires, it is accepted that the letter cannot amount to the same. I have concluded that, had they stopped to think about it at the time, they should have realised this and perhaps sought to put in place a system that allowed them better to evidence their authority to act. Equally, it seems to me that someone in the claimant's position is entitled to be told on what authority he is threatened with entry to his premises.

The protracted period relevant to this case was, as highlighted above, punctuated by periods of inactivity. Nevertheless, in my view the breach must be marked by an award of damages. To mark the breach, the frustration suffered and the repeated failure to comply with the Schedule, I will assess damages as being in the sum of £4,000. This sum is less than I would have awarded if harassment had been established. If established, I would have awarded a sum perhaps nearly double that sum. Aggravated damages arise where the injury to feeling suffered by the claimant is increased by the flagrancy, malevolence, and the nature of any particular unacceptable behaviour on behalf of a defendant. My analysis of the case, set out above, does not allow me to bring this case within the same, and I make no reward in respect of aggravated damages.

For completeness' sake, I have also considered whether an award of exemplary damages is justified. Such damages arise where the court is able to conclude that the established conduct was malicious, oppressive, arbitrary or unconstitutional, and/or where theconduct is calculated by way of profit. The point of such damages is to punish the defendant. Again, on the basis of the analysis set out above, I am unable to conclude that exemplary damages are applicable to this situation.

It follows from my judgment that there will be judgment for the claimant in the sum of £4,000. In ordinary circumstances the issue of interest would arise, which would, in the nature of these damages, be at the rate, I think, of 2 per cent per annum from the date of issueof proceedings.

This transcript has been approved by the
Judge

WAYNE LEIGHTON (Claimant) -v- BRISTOW AND SUTOR (Defendant)

Can be downloaded from:

https://drive.google.com/file/d/1XfplYhSJVNor4MvPkdLQNyeMWpjCD_Dz/view?usp=sharing

ENFORCEMENT AGENTS FINAL NOTICE BEFORE RETUNING ACCOUNT TO THE COUNCIL

Once an enforcement agency realise they are wasting their time trying to collect the council tax arrears they will send you one final notice hoping this will put so much fear in you that you will contact them to setup a payment plan including their fees.

A typical final notice usually states the following:

'Despite all efforts no offer of payment has been forthcoming and the balance of £3576,90 remains outstanding.

We are currently reviewing your cases prior to issuing instructions as to which further method of enforcement we should proceed with. In the first instance we will be instructing our insolvency Solicitors to make a search to check whether you are a property owner in which case we will recommend that a Charging Order be sought incurring additional costs of at least £110 plus the Council's reasonable costs. If you are not a homeowner, we will be recommending to our client that where you are employed an attachment of your earnings is made which we can organise or where you are unemployed and in receipt of benefits, an attachment to your benefits is made.

Alternatively, if any of these methods are not adopted a strong recommendation for our **committal to prison** will be made where further costs of £500+ will be added to the debt.

Should you wish to avoid such proceedings and associated costs then we would recommend you contact us immediately on 0345 601 2692 with your proposals for payment of, if you are suffering genuine financial difficulty.

Jacobs

mail@jacobsenforcement.com

You should have no dealings with the bailiffs, but you should always video them if they visit you. You should also by way of a Subject Access Request to the company request a copy of the bailiffs body cam footage.

Template requesting a copy of their body cam footage sent by email:

Dear Mr Rose,

Today 16.08.2022 I had a visit from two of your agents, they stated their body cam was running. So under a Subject Access Request I am requesting a copy of their footage. I have attached two files with ID.

Yours faithfully,

Name

Your ref: CNR-T XXXX
Acc 3122XXX8

BENEFITS

If you are unemployed the council should take 5% of your monthly Universal Credit. Many councils will use enforcement agents knowing that they will put fear in many council tax debtors and extract from them more than they lawfully can take from Universal Credit.

You should never agree a payment plan with enforcement agents. Only deal and agree to affordable payment plans with the council.

If you are on benefits and want the enforcement agents off your back, email the following template letter to your council. Also downloadable at:

https://docs.google.com/document/d/1rw3HU6hvs_0PPL6TbgCH2RNmUf_-0vyb/edit?usp=sharing&ouid=111889191575252819642&rtpof=true&sd=true

Name
Address
Post Code

8th March 2024

Xxxxx Xxxxxxxxxx Council
Council Tax Enforcement Dept

Formal Request under Regulation 7 Fines Council Tax and Community Charges (Deductions from Universal credit and Other Benefits) Regulations 2013

Re: Council Tax A/c Number xxxxxxxx

Dear Xxxxx Xxxxxxxxxx Council,

I am on Universal Credit which you are well aware of, so my council tax arrears should be taken from my UC. It is my belief that enforcement agents should only be used as a last resort, and not to be used to harass and use threatening behaviour.

It is also my belief that the council are using enforcement agents knowing they will harass and put fear into a person on universal credit to extract more than the lawful 5% the council can take from universal credit.

Third party deductions are fixed at five per cent of Universal Credit Standard Allowance for each third party. This fixed amount cannot be changed.
No more than three third party deductions can be taken at any one time.

Please confirm that all enforcement action will now cease and that my account will be taken back to Xxxxx Xxxxxxxxxx Council revenues.

<u>Council Tax Guidance to local councils on good practice in the collection of Council Tax arrears</u>

3.5 A Local Authority should take all reasonable steps to exhaust other options available to them prior to obtaining a liability order. Once a liability order has been granted a Local Authority should explore other enforcement options which are available to them, <u>such as direct deductions from benefit</u> or an attachment of earnings order.

4.5 Local Authorities should remain prepared to deal directly with individuals at any point.
It is perfectly within their gift to call action back from the bailiffs at any time and where there is a case to do so they should consider such action.

Your faithfully,

Name.

HOMEOWNERS

A Charging Order can be applied for when arrears reaches £1,000
Bankruptcy can be applied for when arrears reach £5,000

The Council Tax (Administration and Enforcement) Regulations 1992

Charging orders

50.—(1) An application to the appropriate court may be made under this regulation where—

(a) a magistrates' court has made a liability order pursuant to regulation 34(6),

(b) the amount mentioned in regulation 34(7)(a) in respect of which the liability order was made is an amount the debtor is liable to pay under Part V, and

(c) at the time that the application under this regulation is made at least £1000 of the amount in respect of which the liability order was made remains outstanding.

(2) The application which may be made to the appropriate court under this regulation is an application by the authority concerned for an order imposing, on any interest held by the debtor beneficially in the relevant dwelling, a charge for securing the due amount; and the court may make such an order on such application.

(3) For the purposes of paragraph (2)—

(a) the authority concerned is the authority which applied for the liability order referred to in paragraph (1)(a),

(b) the relevant dwelling is the dwelling in respect of which, at the time the application for the liability order was made, the debtor was liable to pay council tax,

(c) the due amount is the aggregate of—

(I) an amount equal to any outstanding sum which is or forms part of the amount in respect of which the liability order was made, and

(ii) a sum of an amount equal to the costs reasonably incurred by the applicant in obtaining the charging order,

(d) the appropriate court is the county court for the area in which the relevant dwelling is situated.

The Council Tax (Administration and Enforcement) Regulations 1992

Charging orders: further provision

51.—(1) In deciding whether to make a charging order, the court shall consider all the circumstances of the case, and in particular any evidence before it as to—

(a) the personal circumstances of the debtor, and

(b) whether any other person would be likely to be unduly prejudiced by the making of the order.

(2) A charging order—

(a) shall specify the dwelling concerned and the interest held by the debtor beneficially in it, and

(b) may, as the court thinks fit, be made absolutely or subject to conditions as to the time when the charge is to become enforceable or as to other matters.

(3) A charged imposed by a charging order shall have the like effect and shall be enforceable in the same courts and in the same manner as an equitable charge created by the debtor by writing under his hand.

(4) The court by which a charging order was made may at any time, on the application of the debtor, the authority on whose application the order was made or any person interested in the dwelling, make an order discharging or varying the charging order.

(5) The Land Charges Act 1972(1) and the Land Registration Act 1925(2) shall apply in relation to charging orders as they apply in relation to orders or writs issued or made for the purposes of enforcing judgments; and in section 49(1)(g) of the Land Registration Act 1925, after the words "Local Government Finance Act 1988" there are inserted the words ", or regulations under paragraph 11 of Schedule 4 to the Local Government Finance Act 1992".

(6) Where a charging order has been protected by an entry registered under the Land Charges Act 1972 or the Land Registration Act 1925, an order under paragraph (4) discharging the charging order may direct that the entry be cancelled.

(1) 1972 c. 61; section 6 of the Act was amended by the Supreme Court Act 1981 (c. 54), Schedule 5, and the County Courts Act 1984 (c. 28), Schedule 2, paragraph 18.

(2) 1925 c. 21; section 49(1)(g) was inserted by the Charging Orders Act 1979 (c. 53), section 3(3), and amended by the Drug Trafficking Offences Act 1986 (c. 32), section 39(2), the Criminal Justice Act 1988 (c. 33), Schedule 15, paragraph 6 and regulation 45(5) of the Community Charges (Adminsitration and Enforcement) Regulations 1989 (S.I. 1989/438).

The Council Tax (Administration and Enforcement) Regulations 1992

Insolvency

49.—(1) Where a liability order has been made and the debtor against whom it was made is an individual, the amount due shall be deemed to be a debt for the purposes of section 267 of the Insolvency Act 1986(1) (grounds of creditor's petition).

(2) Where a liability order has been made and the debtor against whom it was made is a company, the amount due shall be deemed to be a debt for the purposes of section 122(1)(f) (winding up of companies by the court) or, as the case may be, section 221(5)(b) (winding up of unregistered companies) of that Act.

(3) For the purposes of this regulation the amount due is an amount equal to any outstanding sum which is or forms part of the amount in respect of which the liability order was made.

COMMITTAL

The Council Tax (Administration and Enforcement) Regulations 1992

Commitment to prison

47.—(1) Where a billing authority has sought to levy an amount by distress under regulation 45, the debtor is an individual who has attained the age of 18 years, and the person making the distress reports to the authority that he was unable (for whatever reason) to find any or sufficient goods of the debtor on which to levy the amount, the authority may apply to a magistrates' court for the issue of a warrant committing the debtor to prison.

(2) On such application being made the court shall (in the debtor's presence) inquire as to his means and inquire whether the failure to pay which has led to the application is due to his wilful refusal or culpable neglect.

(3) If (and only if) the court is of the opinion that his failure is due to his wilful refusal or culpable neglect it may if it thinks fit—

(a) issue a warrant of commitment against the debtor, or

(b) fix a term of imprisonment and postpone the issue of the warrant until such time and on such conditions (if any) as the court thinks just.

(4) The warrant shall be made in respect of the relevant amount; and the relevant amount for this purpose is the aggregate of—

(a) an amount equal to the appropriate amount mentioned in regulation 45(2) or (as the case may be) so much of it as remains outstanding, and

(b) a sum of an amount equal to the costs reasonably incurred by the applicant in respect of the application.

(5) The warrant—

(a) shall state the relevant amount mentioned in paragraph (4),

(b) may be directed to the authority making the application and to such other persons (if any) as the court issuing it thinks fit, and

(c) may be executed anywhere in England by any person to whom it is directed.

(6) If—

(a) before the issue of a warrant the appropriate amount mentioned in regulation 45(2) (or so much of it as remains outstanding) is paid or tendered to the authority, or

(b) after the issue of the warrant, the amount stated in it is paid or tendered to the authority,

the authority shall accept the amount concerned, no further steps shall be taken as regards its recovery, and the debtor if committed to prison shall be released.

(7) The order in the warrant shall be that the debtor be imprisoned for a time specified in the warrant which shall not exceed 3 months, unless the amount stated in the warrant is sooner paid; but—

(a) where a warrant is issued after a postponement under paragraph (3)(b) and, since the term of imprisonment was fixed but before the issue of the warrant, the amount mentioned in paragraph (4)(a) with respect to which the warrant would (but for the postponement) have been made has been reduced by a part payment, the period of imprisonment ordered under the warrant shall be the term fixed under paragraph (3) reduced by such number of days as bears to the total number of days in that term less one day the same proportion as the part paid bears to that amount, and

(b) where, after the issue of a warrant, a part payment of the amount stated in it is made, the period of imprisonment shall be reduced by such number of days as bears to the total number of days in the term of imprisonment specified in the warrant less one day the same proportion as the part paid bears to the amount so stated.

(8) In calculating a reduction required under paragraph (7) any fraction of a day shall be left out of account; and rule 55(1), (2) and (3) of the Magistrates' Courts Rules 1981(1) applies (so far as is relevant) to a part payment as if the imprisonment concerned were

imposed for want of sufficient distress to satisfy a sum adjudged to be paid by a magistrates' court.

The Council Tax (Administration and Enforcement) Regulations 1992

Commitment to prison: further provision

48.—(1) A single warrant may not be issued under regulation 47 against more than one person, and shall be in the form specified as Form C in Schedule 2, or in a form to the like effect.

(2) Where an application under regulation 47 has been made, and after the making of the inquiries mentioned in paragraph (2) of that regulation no warrant is issued or term of imprisonment fixed, the court may remit all or part of the appropriate amount mentioned in regulation 45(2) with respect to which the application related.

(3) Where an application under regulation 47 has been made but no warrant is issued or term of imprisonment fixed, the application may be renewed (except so far as regards any sum remitted under paragraph (2)) on the ground that the circumstances of the debtor have changed.

(4) A statement in writing to the effect that wages of any amount have been paid to the debtor during any period, purporting to be signed by or on behalf of his employer, shall in any proceedings under regulation 47 be evidence of the facts there stated.

(5) For the purpose of enabling inquiry to be made as to the debtor's conduct and means under regulation 47, a justice of the peace may—

(a) issue a summons to him to appear before a magistrates' court and (if he does not obey the summons) issue a warrant for his arrest, or

(b) issue a warrant for the debtor's arrest without issuing a summons.

(6) A warrant issued under paragraph (5) may be executed anywhere in England and Wales by any person to whom it is directed or by any constable acting within his police area; and section 125(3) of the Magistrates' Courts Act 1980 applies to such a warrant.

(7) Regulation 47 and this regulation have effect subject to Part I of the Criminal Justice Act 1982(1) (treatment of young offenders)

Letter from Cornwall Council concerning committal to prison

Revenues and Assessment

Account Reference: 31376444453998
Property Ref:111676549867520
Date: 24 January 2019

Thank you for your email of 04/12/18 with an attached letter dated 30/11/18.

Please find enclosed, as requested, a copy of the Council's recovery policy.

I have also enclosed copies of the liability orders granted against you at BodminMagistrates Court on the 08/04/20 16, 05/08/20 16 and 07/09/20 17 together with relevant copies of the signed pages of the complaint list from each of thesecourts.

I would advise that a financial means test is not required when the Local Authority requests the Magistrates Court to grant a liability order. As the name suggests the Court is only required to make a decision about whether the person is liable to pay the Council Tax billed in order for them to grant a liability order. However, when a committal summons has been issued the Magistrates will conduct a means enquiry at the hearing to determine if willful refusal or culpable neglect has been proven.

As you are aware, last year we considered your application for a reduction in accordance with Section 13A (1) (c)of the 1992 Local Government Finance Act as amended by section 10 of the Local Government Finance Act 2012 and the decisionwas not to reduce your council tax charge. The reasons we gave you for this were

Previous correspondence proves that you are unwilling to pay your council tax as oppose to being unable to pay.

You have not provided any evidence to support your statement that your financial situation is the reason you are not paying your council tax.

If your income is at a level where you cannot afford your council tax you shouldbe claiming council tax support and also housing benefit to assist you with the payment of your rent.

If the charge was reduced to zero, there is little likelihood of you paying your council tax for future years.There can be no justification for increasing the burden on other local council taxpayers by funding a reduction on this account.

The situation remains the same now as it was then.

After obtaining liability orders, on each occasion we have invited you to provide details of your financial situation so that we could take that into account when deciding our next course of action but unfortunately you failed to complete and return the forms wesent to you so we have never received any details of your financial situation.

As previously advised a financial means test is not required in order to obtain a liabilityorder although it is required as part of the committal proceedings process so you will be requested to provide this to the Court, should a committal summons be issued against you.

While you may not like or agree with the council tax legislation, the action we aretaking is in accordance with it and it will ultimately be up to the Court to make a decision.
An arrest warrant would be issued against you if you are summonsed to attend a committal court hearing and you failed to attend. I have listed answers to the pointsyou raise regarding this as follows:-

The Warrant could be executed at any location within England and Wales apart fromgovernment barracks or military buildings.

The warrant can be executed at any location within England and Wales apart fromgovernment buildings or military barracks.

- see the following link http://www.leqislation.Nov.uk/ukpga/2004/28/schedule/4

If the warrant includes the word "Constable alongside Marston/Approved Officerthen the police can assist with the arrest. Currently the warrants issued by Cornwall Magistrates Court do not include the word ' Constable ' .

The debtors consent is not required to execute the warrant, however police assistance would be required if the debtor was non-compliant.

The complaint for committal would be made under oath.

The warrant remains live until it is withdrawn by a judge or Magistrate.

I would refer you to the Prison Service to answer this question.

Should you be given a prison sentence and you serve this sentence, the total debtincluded on the committal summons will be discharged.

Should you serve the prison sentence as imposed by the Magistrates, the totalbalance on the committal summons would be written-off.

The letter you were sent gives you an opportunity to liaise with the Council to make an arrangement to pay your Council Tax arrears without the need for committal action tobe taken. It is not too late to do this - please contact us to discuss an arrangement to pay. This would negate the need to issue a committal summons.

I can confirm that I am not legally trained and I am not a registered practising solicitor but I am authorised to represent Cornwall Council in the Magistrates Court as a Revenues Court Officer in connection with proceedings relating to the recovery of Council Tax, Business Rates and Business Improvement District levy.

Yours sincerely

Adrian Walters
Revenues Court
Officer
Revenues and Assessment (Customer Access and Digital Services)

At the first threat from the local authority of committal to prison the following template should be emailed to the local authorities Revenues Court Officer, who is an employee or the council and not the court.

Dear Sir/Madam,

Thank you for your letter dated xx.xx.xxxx

I am shocked that in these times of hardship when people are struggling to pay utility bills and put food on the table, you are sending out letters threatening imprisonment.

It's clear that it is too late to now conduct any financial means test as stated in **Lloyd & 44 Others.**

'The applicants further referred to the above-cited domestic case of R. v. Leeds City Justices ex parte Kennett to submit **that it was a condition precedent for the magistrates to inquire into the circumstances of an applicant at the time at which each liability order was made.'**

At this stage, it would be deemed to be unlawful if I were to be imprisoned, because one reason being at no stage have the magistrates ever undertaken a means inquiry at the time of making each liability order against me.

Yours faithfully,

Name.

Emails Concerning The Threat of Committal To Prison And Replies

From: Paul Patterson <paulstroketalk@aol.com>
Sent: 15 October 2021 19:44
To: cornwall-admin <cornwall-admin@Justice.gov.uk>
Cc: adrian.walters@cornwall.gov.uk

Subject: Notice of new date of hearing Case No: 502100231045

Dear Sir/Madam,

Can you please confirm the date for the non payment of council tax which was originally to be heard on 6th October 2021

Mrs L Ryan Revenues Court Officer for the council has informed me it has been adjourned until 17/11/2021 (summons No:204378) case number 502100231045 and yet the court has informed me the date of this hearing is 15/12/2021.

The court has also informed me of a second case at the same time case number 502100231045/1 which is a complaint for **committal to prison** for non- payment of council tax and costs of £473.91. **The council have not informed me of this second complaint.**

As I have not received a summons for committal to prison can you please send me copies of the following:
1. Copy of the complaint laid to the magistrates for a committal summons to be granted, a signed copy of the complaint having being granted.
2. Copy of the summons for committal.
3. Copy of the complaint laid to the magistrates for a summons to be granted for non payment of council tax.

Yours faithfully,
Paul Patterson.

From: Paul Patterson <paulstroketalk@aol.com>
Sent: 18 October 2021 12:56

To: cornwall-admin <cornwall-admin@Justice.gov.uk>
Cc: adrian.walters@cornwall.gov.uk
Subject: Re: Notice of new date of hearing Case No: 502100231045

Dear Debby,

Can you confirm the court hearing is for a **COMMITTAL TO PRISON** hearing as stated on the Notice of new date hearing from the court, if so I ask again for:

1. Copy of the complaint laid to the magistrates for a committal summons to be granted, a signed copy of the complaint having being granted.

2. Copy of the summons for committal.

3. Copy of the complaint laid to the magistrates for a summons to be granted for non payment of council tax.

Yours faithfully,

Paul Patterson.

-----Original Message-----

From: cornwall-admin <cornwall-admin@Justice.gov.uk>

To: paulstroketalk@aol.com <paulstroketalk@aol.com>

CC: adrian.walters@cornwall.gov.uk <adrian.walters@cornwall.gov.uk>

Sent: Mon, 18 Oct 2021 12:26

Subject: RE: Notice of new date of hearing Case No: 502100231045

Good Morning

Thank you for your email. I conform the date of your court hearing os set for the

15th December at Truro Magistrates Court at 10.30am.

I will defer to Mr Walters at Cornwall Council to reply to the further requests made with in

your email.

With regards

Mrs Debby Eastley

Court Support Officer

From: Paul Patterson <paulstroketalk@aol.com>
Sent: 18 October 2021 12:56
To: cornwall-admin <cornwall-admin@Justice.gov.uk>
Cc: adrian.walters@cornwall.gov.uk
Subject: Re: Notice of new date of hearing Case No: 502100231045

Dear Debby,

Can you confirm the court hearing is for a COMMITTAL TO PRISON hearing as stated on the Notice of new date hearing from the court, if so I ask again for:

1. Copy of the complaint laid to the magistrates for a committal summons to be granted, a signed copy of the complaint having being granted.

2. Copy of the summons for committal.

3. Copy of the complaint laid to the magistrates for a summons to be granted for non payment of council tax.

Yours faithfully,

Paul Patterson.

Eastley, Debby
From:debby.eastley@justice.gov.uk

To:Paul Patterson
Mon, 18 Oct 2021 at 13:05

Mr Patterson

The listing for the 15th December is a Complaint for a **Committal to Prison for Non Payment of Council** and I ask that you wait for Mr Walters to provide the relevant copies that you have requested, I have copied him into my responses to you.

With continued best regards.

Mrs Debby Eastley
Court Support Officer

cornwall-admin
From:cornwall-admin@justice.gov.uk
Tue, 19 Oct 2021 at 10:56
Dear Mr Patterson

Thank you for your email below. Due to an administration error your case was listed for the incorrect type of hearing. Your case has now been rearranged for the Cornwall Council to apply for a liability order for council tax owed.

I am sorry for the distress that this has caused you.

Your sincerely

Mr Rutherford
Administrative Officer

The case law which has all the evidence that to imprison you would be unlawful

COUR EUROPÉENNE DES DROITS DE L'HOMME EUROPEAN COURT OF HUMAN RIGHTS

FOURTH SECTION DECISION

AS TO THE ADMISSIBILITY OF

Application nos. 29798/96 and others by Raymond LLOYD and 44 others against the United Kingdom

Mr M. PELLONPÄÄ, *President*, Sir Nicolas BRATZA,
MrsV.STRÁŽNICKÁ
Mr R. MARUSTE,
Mr S. PAVLOVSCHI,
Mr L. GARLICKI,
Mr J. BORREGO BORREGO, *judges*,
and Mr M. O'BOYLE, *Section Registrar*,

Having regard to the above applications lodged with the European Commission of Human Rights and the European Court of Human Rights on various dates from 6 November 1995 to 7 July 1999,

Having regard to Article 5 § 2 of Protocol No. 11 to the Convention, by which the competence to examine the applications that were originally lodged with the European Commission of Human Rights was transferred to the Court, Having regard to the observations submitted by the respondent Government and the observations in reply submitted by the applicants,

Having deliberated, decides as follows:

THE FACTS

The applicants are United Kingdom nationals. Raymond Lloyd (application no. 29798/96) is represented before the Court by Chamberlins Solicitors, lawyers practising in Hertfordshire; Kenneth Wood (application no. 30395/96) is represented by Mr C. McKay, a lawyer practising in Grimsby; Robert Waller (application no.

34327/96) is represented by Mr T. Humpage, a lawyer practising in Ipswich; G.M. (application no. 34341/96) is represented by Ms G. Christie, a lawyer practising in County Durham; Anthony Townsend (application no. 42039/98) is represented by Ms D. Still, a lawyer practising in Newcastle-upon-Tyne; Mark Wood (application no. 47441/99) is represented by Ms H. Dent, a lawyer practising in Lancashire; the remaining applicants are represented by Dicksons HMB Solicitors, lawyers practising in Stoke-on-Trent. The circumstances of the cases

The facts of the cases, as submitted by the parties, may be summarised as follows.

Each applicant failed to pay sums due in respect of either local taxes (community charge, council tax or non-domestic rates), or court-imposed fines. In respect of the failure to pay local taxes, the magistrates' court had in each case determined that the applicants were liable to pay (issuing a "liability order"); in fines cases, the magistrates' court had imposed the fine as the sentence following a criminal conviction.

Each applicant fell into arrears with the payments due from them. These cases involve the enforcement proceedings in respect of their arrears in the magistrates' court. Each applicant appeared before the court, following the issuing of an application for their committal to prison as a result of their failure to pay the sums due. At that hearing the magistrates found that the non-payment was due to the applicant's wilful refusal or culpable neglect. As a result each applicant was sentenced to a period of imprisonment. The sentence was either imposed immediately (G.M., application no. 34341/96) or was suspended on terms that the applicant make periodic payments towards the outstanding sum. In the latter circumstances, when the applicant failed to comply with the terms imposed, a further hearing was held in the magistrates' court at which the suspended term of imprisonment was activated. Each applicant spent a period of time in prison. Legal aid (free legal representation where the applicant did not have sufficient means to pay for it) was not available for these enforcement proceedings prior to 1 June 1997 and none of the applicants were legally represented at the hearings in front of the magistrates.

Following their imprisonment, an application was made on behalf of each applicant, by way of either judicial review or case stated, which resulted in the High Court quashing the orders made by the magistrates. The majority of the applicants were released from prison on bail at the time of making their applications to the High Court. In three cases the orders of the magistrates were quashed in a judgment of the High Court. In the remaining cases the orders were quashed following the High Court's approval of a consent order agreed between the applicants and the magistrates who had sentenced them.

With one exception [Christison (56429/00)], the Court has set out the relevant facts pertaining to each applicant in the table which appears at the end of this decision. That table sets out the following information in respect of each applicant: their name and application number; whether their case involved non-payment of community charge ("CC"), council tax ("CT"), non-domestic rates ("NDR") or fines ("F") and the number of days which they spent in prison; whether their proceedings in the magistrates' court took place before or after legal aid became available on 1 June 1997; and the grounds upon which the High Court quashed the orders of the magistrates. Additional relevant factual information appears in this column of the table where appropriate.

Where the orders of the magistrates were quashed following a judgment, the Court has indicated that fact in the table and quoted from the relevant part of the judgment. Where the orders of the magistrates were quashed by means of a consent order, the Court has set out the terms of the consent order in full. In such cases, where the terms agreed contain obvious mistakes or misquotations from domestic case-law, the Court has inserted corrections in square brackets. However, where it is not obvious what the relevant correction should be, the Court has simply left the order in its original form.

Throughout the text of this decision, where there is a reference to a specific applicant, the Court has set out the surname of the applicant followed by their application number in brackets. The words "justices" and "magistrates" are synonymous in domestic law.

For reasons of space, the Court sets out the facts of the Christison (56429/00) application below.

Allison CHRISTISON (56429/00)

This applicant's application for judicial review was determined by the judgment of Mr Justice Collins in *R. v. Doncaster Justices ex parte Christison and Jack* (13 May 1999). It is clear from that judgment that the applicant was summoned to court as a result of her failure to pay council tax. On 21 January 1998 the justices, having neither received any evidence about, nor asked any questions about, the financial outgoings of the applicant, found her to have culpably neglected to pay the council tax and made an order imposing 28 days' imprisonment suspended on payment of £8 per month.

The applicant did not make the payments in compliance with the magistrates' order of 21 January 1998. She was therefore summoned to appear on 1 June 1998 for the magistrates' court to determine whether the warrant of committal should be issued. The justices were told by the prosecutor that the applicant had been served with the notice of the hearing three weeks prior to the hearing. They proceeded in her absence and issued the committal warrant. She spent a total of two days in prison.

The order of 21 January 1998 was quashed by Mr Justice Collins on the following ground:

> "[N]o proper means enquiry was carried out ... The Justices accept that there was no proper means enquiry and, therefore, the order is going to be quashed. (...)
>
> ... Justices probably carry out means enquiries every day. They must know, and if they do not, their clerks should advise them, what ought to be asked and what information ought to be obtained. They failed to do that in [this] case."

The order of 1 June 1998 was quashed by Mr Justice Collins for the following reasons:

> "...The time has come to try to make it abundantly clear to Justices that, in the view of this court, it is difficult to conceive that there will be circumstances which justify the making of a committal order when the defendant fails to appear before the court. It means that the Justices are unable to ascertain whether there are, in truth, reasons why payment has not been made which might excuse such payment, and furthermore, reasons why in an individual case it would be wrong to send the person immediately to prison. Alternatively, it might be proper to reduce the period of imprisonment that is considered appropriate, if any is considered appropriate. It may transpire that by the time that the question of implementing the suspended committal order is considered, the circumstances of the defendant have changed. Whereas before she might have been able to pay perhaps, through illness or whatever reason, by now she cannot. Thus, it would be wrong to commit her. Committal, I must re-emphasise,

> can only occur if the Justices are satisfied that there is a continuing wilful refusal or culpable neglect.
>
> The Justices have a perfectly sensible and powerful weapon available to them to deal with cases where a defendant does not attend, and that is a Warrant Not Backed for Bail. That is the means by which a person can be brought before the court and made to explain why he or she has not paid. Then the Justices will have the proper information before them to enable them to decide whether the committal is indeed correct. I cannot emphasise strongly enough my view that Justices should not, unless there are very exceptional circumstances (such as positive evidence that a defendant is refusing to attend and has expressed an unwillingness to comply with the court order) commit to prison in the absence of a defendant. ...
>
> It is true that in these cases, the Justices were told that service had been effected, but service some three weeks before is nothing to the point. Much can happen in that time... Furthermore, there was no evidence put before the Justices to support the contention that service had been effected, and for my part I do not think it right, when someone's liberty is at stake, for Justices to rely upon the word of the prosecutor unsupported by any evidence.
>
> A civil court which commits for contempt, which may be contempt occasioned by failure to comply with a court order, requires proof of service and that is usually done by a bailiff or whoever, indicating that service has been effected. It seems to me that it is quite wrong that Justices should put up with a lesser standard than that."

Mr Justice Collins also awarded costs against the justices on the following basis:

> "It is unusual for costs to be awarded against Justices who do not attend applications against them for judicial review. The principle which is applied has recently been referred to by Latham J in *R. v. Newcastle-upon-Tyne Justices ex parte Devine* (1998) RA 97. At page 104 of the report, the learned judge refers to a decision of the Divisional Court, *R. v. York City Justices ex parte Farmery* 153 JP 257, the head note of which reads:
>
>> '... the court would be guided by the principles set out in *R. v. Willesden Justices, ex parte Roberts* (1960) 124 JP 336 wherein it was decided respectively:
>> (i) that costs would only be awarded against Justices in the rarest of circumstances when they have done something

which calls for strong disapproval; and (ii) that it was the practice not to grant costs against Justices merely because they have made a mistake in law, but only if they have acted perversely or with some disregard for the elementary principles which every court ought to obey, and even then only if it was a flagrant instance.' (...)

... In [this] case the committal took place in the absence of the defendant.

This court has made it clear that Justices must be satisfied, at the very least, that there has been proper service, and, as I have said, I find it very difficult to conceive of circumstances which would justify a committal in the absence of a defendant. Thus it seems to me that the conduct of these Justices can properly be said to fall within the description that I have set out and which is referred to in the *Newcastle* case by Latham J."

Relevant domestic law

Appeal from a decision of a magistrates' court by way of case stated

By virtue of section 111 of the Magistrates' Courts Act 1980 a party to proceedings before a magistrates' court may "question the proceeding on the ground that it is wrong in law or is in excess of jurisdiction by applying to the justices composing the court to state a case for the opinion of the High Court on the question of law or jurisdiction involved ...". This is known as the "case stated" procedure.

Under section 113 of the 1980 Act, magistrates may grant bail to a party who applies to them to state a case; but if they refuse to do so, in cases categorised as "civil" under the domestic law, the High Court has no jurisdiction to grant bail until it is seized of some substantive proceedings to which the grant of bail can be ancillary.

Judicial review

According to Halsbury's Laws of England, Fourth Edition, Volume 1(1) at paragraph 59:

"Judicial review is the process by which the High Court exercises its supervisory jurisdiction over the proceedings and decisions of inferior courts, tribunals and other bodies or persons who carry out quasi-judicial functions or who are charged with the performance of public acts and duties ...

Judicial review is concerned with reviewing not the merits of the decision in respect of which the application for judicial review is made, but the decision making process itself ...

The duty of the court is to confine itself to the question of legality. Its concern is with whether a decision making authority exceeded its powers, committed an error of law, committed a breach of the rules of natural justice, reached a decision which no reasonable tribunal could have reached or abused its powers."

The distinction between an act of a magistrates' court which is merely wrong in law and one which is so wrong as to be in excess of jurisdiction

The principles underlying the domestic law as set out under this heading are largely as previously stated in the case-law of the Convention organs, in particular in the judgments of the Court in the cases of *Benham v. the United Kingdom* (judgment of 10 June 1996, *Reports of Judgments and Decisions* 1996-III, p. 738) ("*Benham*"), and *Perks and Others v. the United Kingdom* nos. 25277/94 and others, 12 October 1999 ("*Perks*"). The Government submitted that this was an accurate statement of the position under domestic law. The applicants disagreed and the extent to which they did so can be seen by reference to the applicants' arguments as set out under the below heading "Preliminary submission that *Benham* and *Perks* were wrongly decided".

In English law, orders of a magistrates' court which are in excess of jurisdiction are void from the outset, whereas orders made within jurisdiction remain valid until set aside by a superior court. It is only in respect of the former type of error that a court can be held civilly liable in damages (under section 108 of the Courts and Legal Services Act 1990, which replaced section 45 of the Justices of the Peace Act 1979 – see below).

The appropriate test for whether an order of a magistrates' court is void for lack of jurisdiction is that set out by the House of Lords in *McC. v. Mullan* [1984] 3 All England Reports 908. In that case magistrates had made an order sending a 14-year-old boy to a training school after a hearing at which he was not legally represented, had not applied for legal aid and had not been informed of his right so to do. The order was quashed on judicial review on the ground that, by virtue of Article 15(1) of the Treatment of Offenders (Northern Ireland) Order 1976, magistrates were not permitted to pass a custodial sentence for the first time on a juvenile who was not legally represented, unless he had applied for legal aid and had been refused on grounds of means or had been informed of his right to apply for it but had refused or neglected to do so.

The boy then applied for damages for false imprisonment against the magistrates. Since the case was decided prior to the enactment of the Courts and Legal Services Act 1990 and at a time when magistrates were liable in damages for false imprisonment if they acted in excess of jurisdiction, the House of Lords was required to decide the jurisdictional question. Indeed, Lord Templeman in his judgment stated as follows:

> "The question to be determined on this appeal is whether the magistrates acted within their jurisdiction or without jurisdiction."

In addressing that question, Lord Bridge specifically referred to the case of *Anisminic Ltd. v. the Foreign Compensation Commisison* [1969] 2 Appeal Cases 147 (HL) ("*Anisminic*") and stated as follows:

> "I do not believe that the novel test of excess of jurisdiction which emerges from the *Anisminic* case, ... however valuable it may be in ensuring that the supervisory jurisdiction of the superior courts over inferior tribunals is effective to secure compliance with the law and is not lightly to be ousted by statute, has any application whatever to the construction of s[ection] 15 of the 1964 Northern Ireland Act or s[ection] 45 of the 1979 [Justices of the Peace] Act."

In the judgment of the House of Lords, a magistrates' court acted in excess of jurisdiction in three circumstances only: (1) if it acted without having jurisdiction over the cause, (2) if it exercised its powers in a procedural manner that involved a gross and obvious irregularity, or (3) if it made an order that had no proper foundation in law because of a failure to observe a statutory condition precedent. The instant case fell within the third limb of the rule: the magistrates were liable in damages because they had not observed the requirements of Article 15(1) of the 1976 Order. As such, they had failed to fulfil the statutory condition precedent to the imposition of the sentence of detention.

During the course of his judgment, Lord Bridge commented on the jurisdiction of magistrates in conducting a criminal trial:

> "... once justices have duly entered upon a summary trial of a matter within their jurisdiction, only something quite exceptional occurring in the course of their proceeding to a determination can oust their jurisdiction ... [A]n error (whether of law or fact) in deciding a collateral issue on which jurisdiction depends will not

do so. Nor will the absence of any evidence to support a conviction ..."

Lord Bridge also said the following in relation to the second situation set out above in which a magistrates' court acted in excess of jurisdiction:

"Justices would, of course, be acting 'without jurisdiction or in excess of jurisdiction' within the meaning of s[ection] 15 if, in the course of hearing a case within their jurisdiction, they were guilty of some gross and obvious irregularity of procedure, as for example if one justice absented himself for part of the hearing and relied on another to tell him what had happened during his absence, or of the rules of natural justice, as for example if the justices refused to allow the defendant to give evidence. But I would leave for determination if and when they arise other more subtle cases one might imagine in which it could successfully be contended in judicial review proceedings that a conviction was vitiated on some narrow technical ground involving a procedural irregularity or even a breach of the rules of natural justice. Such convictions, if followed by a potential trespass to person or goods, would not, in my opinion, necessarily expose the justices to liability in damages."

The final limb of the rule formulated by the House of Lords in *McC. v. Mullan* (that is, that magistrates exceed their jurisdiction when they make an order which has no foundation in law because of a failure to observe a statutory condition precedent) was applied by the Court of Appeal in
R. v. Manchester City Magistrates' Court, ex parte Davies [1989] 1 All England Reports 90, a case concerning rates (a local tax which was the predecessor to the community charge). In the course of his judgment in that case, Lord Justice O'Connor stated:

"I return to the issue under s[ection] 45 of the 19[7]9 Act. This section was considered by the House of Lords in *McC. v. Mullan* ... That was a case from Northern Ireland but the relevant statutory provisions are the same."

Again, the issue was whether magistrates had acted in excess of jurisdiction and were therefore liable in damages for false imprisonment. In considering that question Lord Justice Neill stated as follows:

"It is to be noted that in *Anisminic Ltd. v. the Foreign Compensation Commission* ... Lord Reid expressed the opinion that it is better not to use the term [jurisdiction] 'except in the narrow and original sense of the tribunal being entitled to enter on the inquiry in question'. It is plain, however, that in s[ection]

> 45(1) 'jurisdiction' has a wider meaning than this original meaning."

The plaintiff had been unable to pay all of the rates for which he became liable in December 1984, and in January 1986 he failed to follow his accountant's advice to close his business and elect bankruptcy. Applying legislation similar to regulation 41 of the Community Charge Regulations (for which, see below), the magistrates found that his failure to follow the accountant's advice constituted culpable neglect and they committed him to prison. The Court of Appeal held that no causal connection had been established between the failure to follow the advice in 1986 and the failure to pay the rates in 1984; and that the magistrates had not properly entered into the inquiry as to whether the failure to pay was due to culpable neglect, which was required by the legislation as a statutory condition precedent to the exercise by the justices of their power to issue a warrant of commitment. They were therefore acting in excess of jurisdiction and were liable in damages.

The three Appeal Court judges expressed their findings in slightly different terms. Lord Justice O'Connor observed that "they never carried out the inquiry required [by the law]". Lord Justice Neill found that "some inquiry about the applicant's finances was made", but that "a clear and crucial distinction can be drawn between the inquiry required by the statute and the inquiry which was in fact carried out. The justices never examined the question whether *failure to pay* was due to culpable neglect ... In my judgment, the statutory inquiry was not held in the present case"; and Sir Roger Ormrod (who dissented from the majority decision) said: "... it is quite clear that the justices carried out an inquiry into means carefully and in detail ... It is equally plain that they misdirected themselves completely ... They ... failed to realise that the question they had to decide was whether the applicant's failure to pay his rates was '*due* either to his wilful refusal or to his culpable neglect' ".

Statutory provisions

Provisions concerning enforcement of payment of the community charge, council tax and non-domestic rates

The relevant subordinate legislation is the Community Charge (Administration and Enforcement) Regulations 1989 (Statutory Instrument 1989/438) ("the 1989 Regulations").

The relevant provisions of regulation 29 ("application for a liability order") are as follows:

"(1) If an amount which has fallen due ... is wholly or partly unpaid the charging authority may ... apply to a magistrates' court for an order against the person by whom it is payable. ...The court shall make the order if it is satisfied that the sum has become payable by the defendant and has not been paid."

Regulation 39(1) provides for the seizure and sale of a debtor's property ("levying of distress"):

> "Where a liability order has been made the authority which applied for the order may levy the appropriate amount by distress and sale of goods of the debtor against whom the order was made."

Regulation 41 is concerned with the committal to prison of a debtor, and provides, so far as is relevant: "(1) Where a charging authority has sought to levy an amount by distress under regulation 39, the debtor is an individual, and it appears to the authority that no (or insufficient) goods of the debtor can be found on which to levy the amount, the authority may apply to a magistrates' court for the issue of a warrant committing the debtor to prison.

> On such application being made the court shall (in the debtor's presence) inquire as to his means and inquire whether the failure to pay which led to the liability order concerned being made against him was due to his wilful refusal or culpable neglect.

> If (and only if) the court is of the opinion that his failure was due to his wilful refusal or culpable neglect it may if it thinks fit -

> issue a warrant of commitment against the debtor, or

> fix a term of imprisonment and postpone the issue of the warrant until such time and on such conditions (if any) as the court thinks just. ...

(7) The order in the warrant shall be that the debtor be imprisoned for a time specified in the warrant which shall not exceed 3 months, unless the amount stated in the warrant is sooner paid"

Regulation 42 makes further provision in respect of committal to prison. It provides, in relevant part, as follows:

> "(2) Where an application under regulation 41 has been made, and after the making of the inquiries mentioned in paragraph (2) of that regulation no warrant is issued or term of imprisonment fixed, the court may remit all or part of the appropriate amount

mentioned in regulation 39(2) with respect to which the application related.

(3) Where an application under regulation 41 has been made but no warrant is issued or term of imprisonment fixed, the application may be renewed (except so far as regards any sum remitted under paragraph (2)) on the ground that the circumstances of the debtor have changed."

Regulations 47 and 48 of the Council Tax (Administration and Enforcement) Regulations 1992 (Statutory Instrument 1992/613) and regulations 16 and 17 of the Non-Domestic Rating (Collection and Enforcement) (Local Lists) Regulations 1989 (Statutory Instrument 1989/1058), which concern the commitment to prison of a person for failure to pay council tax and non-domestic rates respectively, are in similar terms to regulations 41 and 42 of the 1989 Regulations.

Provisions concerning enforcement of payment of fines

Sections 77(2) and 82 of the Magistrates' Courts Act 1980 read, in relevant part, as follows:

"77. Postponement of issue of warrant.

Where a magistrates' court has power to issue a warrant of commitment under this Part of this Act, it may, if it thinks it expedient to do so, fix a term of imprisonment and postpone the issue of the warrant until such time and on such conditions, if any, as the court thinks just."

"82. Restriction on power to impose imprisonment for default

Where on the occasion of the offender's conviction a magistrates' court does not issue a warrant of commitment for a default in paying any... sum [adjudged to be paid following conviction] ... or fix a term of imprisonment under ... section 77(2) which is to be served by him in the event of any such default, it shall not thereafter issue a warrant of commitment for any such default or for want of sufficient distress to satisfy such a sum unless - (...)

(b) The court has since the conviction inquired into his means in his presence on at least one occasion.

Where a magistrates' court is required by subsection (3) above to inquire into a person's means, the court may not on the occasion of the inquiry or at any time thereafter issue a warrant of commitment for a default in paying any such sum unless - (...)

The court is satisfied that the default is due to the offender's wilful refusal or culpable neglect; and

has considered or tried all other methods of enforcing payment of the sum and it appears to the court that they are inappropriate or unsuccessful."

Section 82(4A) lists the methods of enforcing payment that are mentioned in the above-cited subsection 82(4)(b)(ii). One such method that is listed in section 82(4A) is the imposition of a 'fines supervision order' under section 88 of the Magistrates' Courts Act. Section 82 continues:

"(5) After the occasion of an offender's conviction by a magistrates' court, the court shall not, unless -

the court has previously fixed a term of imprisonment under section 77(2) above which is to be served by the offender in the event of a default in paying a sum adjudged to be paid by the conviction; (...)

issue a warrant of commitment for a default in paying the sum or fix such a term except at a hearing at which the offender is present.

(5A) A magistrates' court may not issue a warrant of commitment under subsection (5) above at a hearing at which the offender is not present unless the clerk of the court has first served on the offender a notice in writing stating that the court intends to hold a hearing to consider whether to issue such a warrant and giving the reason why the court so intends. (...)

(5F) A notice under subsection (5A) above to be served on any person shall be deemed to be served on that person if it is sent by registered post or the recorded delivery service addressed to him at his last known address, notwithstanding that the notice is returned as undelivered or is for any other reason not received by that person.

Where a magistrates' court issues a warrant of commitment on the ground that one of the conditions mentioned in subsection (1) or (4) above is satisfied, it shall state that fact, specifying the ground, in the warrant."

Restrictions on imposing custodial sentences on persons under the age of 21

Part I of the Criminal Justice Act 1982 sets out provisions in relation to the custody and detention of persons under 21 years of age. Section 1 reads, in relevant part, as follows:

"1. General restriction on custodial sentences

No court shall commit a person under 21 years of age to be detained under section 9 below [Detention of persons aged 18-20 for default or contempt] unless it is of the opinion that no other method of dealing with him is appropriate; (...)

(5A) Where a magistrates' court commits a person under 21 years of age to be detained under section 9 below, it shall -

state in open court the reason for its opinion that no other method of dealing with him is appropriate; and

cause that reason to be specified in the warrant of commitment and to be entered in the register."

Section 3 of the Criminal Justice Act 1982 reads, in relevant part, as follows:

"3. Restriction on imposing custodial sentences on persons under 21 not legally represented. -

A magistrates' court on summary conviction or the Crown Court on committal for sentence or on conviction on indictment shall not -

pass a sentence of detention in a young offender institution (...)

in respect of or on a person who is not legally represented in that court, unless either -

he applied for legal aid and the application was refused on the ground that it did not appear his means were such that he required assistance; or

having been informed of his right to apply for legal aid and had the opportunity to do so, he refused or failed to apply."

Regulation 42(7) of the 1989 Regulations states that the above sections of the Criminal Justice Act 1982 apply to proceedings under regulation 41 of the 1989 Regulations.

Case-law

Among the further case-law referred to in the judgments and consent orders of the High Court, and/or referred to by the parties in their submissions, was the following:

The inquiry into the debtor's means and circumstances

General

In *R. v. Hyndburn Justices ex parte Derrick Long* (18 October 1993), Mr Justice Schiemann stated as follows in a case concerning the non- payment of the community charge:

> " ... It is important when dealing with the liberty of citizens only to set in train the process of imprisonment when all the requirements imposed by law have been carefully considered. It is important to note that, in this field as in the case of suspended sentences of imprisonment imposed pursuant to the criminal law, the same degree of care must be exercised in the case of a suspended penalty as in the case of an immediate penalty."

Failure to hold a proper means inquiry

In *R. v. Woking Justices ex parte Johnstone* [1942] 2 King's Bench 248, the Divisional Court, in examining legislation in similar terms to the 1989 Regulations, emphasised that, in order to commit to prison, the justices, following their inquiry, had to be of the opinion that the failure to pay was due either to wilful refusal or culpable neglect.

In *R. v. Stafford Justices ex parte Shaun Thomas Johnson* (16 March 1995) Mr Justice Laws stated as follows:

> **"... The means inquiry required by regulation 41(2) is of great importance because without it the Justices plainly cannot properly arrive at a conclusion as to whether the failure to pay had been due to the debtor's wilful refusal or culpable neglect. A means inquiry, thus, is at the centre of the enforcement procedure which is laid down by these Regulations. These Justices did not, in truth, embark upon a proper means inquiry at all. It follows that their order committing the applicant to prison is entirely vitiated."**

In *Meara v. DPP* (25 November 1998), a case involving the non-payment of fines, Lord Justice Rose stated that:

> "... an essential prerequisite to a finding of culpable neglect must be the holding of a full means inquiry".

Failure to examine each liability order separately

In *R. v. Leeds Justices ex parte Kennett* [1996] Rating and Valuation Reporter ("RVR") 53, an order committing the applicant to prison for non- payment of community charge following the issue of three liability orders in respect of non-payment for the years 1990-91, 1991-92 and 1992-93 was quashed as a full means inquiry in respect of each liability order had not been made under regulation 41(2) of the 1989 Regulations. Mr Justice Owen stated as follows during the course of his judgment:

> "It is apparent from the wording of the Regulations that each liability order is to be considered separately and in respect of each liability order there has to be, as I see it, a decision as to whether there was wilful refusal or culpable neglect shown."

The above conclusion was followed by Mr Justice Dyson in *R. v Durham City Justices ex parte Fleming* [1997] RVR 244 at 246; by Mr Justice Keene in *R. v. Gloucestershire Justices ex parte Daldry* [2001] RVR 242 at 243; and by Mr Justice Gage in *R. v. Sheffield Justices ex parte Broadhurst* [2001] RVR 245 at 246.

The burden of proof

In *R. v. South Tyneside Justices ex parte Stuart Daniel Martin* (31 July 1995), Mr Justice Sedley stated the following in respect of the burden of proof:

> "... It is necessary in my judgment for Justices to be satisfied not merely on the balance of probability but so that they are sure, following a proper means inquiry, that the debtor's failure to pay has been due to his or her wilful refusal or culpable neglect to pay, before they can issue a warrant of commitment or fix a term of imprisonment and postpone the issue of the warrant...
>
> If I am wrong in this, and if the proper standard is a civil standard, what is at stake for the individual makes it inescapable that only the highest standard of probability is commensurate with the exercise of the power of committal or of fixing a term of imprisonment.
>
> **The Justices, on advice, applied neither such standard.**
>
> In my judgment a bare balance of probability is not a sufficient standard and their decisions of 6th April 1993 and 27th July 1993 to fix terms of imprisonment and postpone the issue of warrants of committal on grounds of culpable neglect cannot therefore stand."

Mr Justice Sedley concluded as follows:

> "... To be open to criticism for the disposal of slender resources is one thing; to be guilty of culpable neglect in the disposal of them is another.
>
> In my judgment the first fixing of the term of imprisonment and the postponement of the warrant were done after a means inquiry too perfunctory to constitute compliance with Regulation 41(2). The fixing of a separate term of imprisonment and the postponement of the warrant in July 1993, although it followed a much fuller inquiry, was again carried out on the basis of data which were not capable by themselves of founding a finding of culpable neglect to pay, whether on the lower standard of proof that was applied or on the higher standard which, as I have held, ought to have been applied. Accordingly the applicant succeeds in his application to quash both decisions of the Justices".

In the case of *R. v. Mid Herts Justices ex parte Cox* (19 October 1995) Mr Justice Laws expressly agreed with what Mr Justice Sedley had said in relation to the burden of proof in the above *Martin* case.

The consideration of alternatives to imprisonment

Failure to pay local taxes

In *R. v. the Alfreton Magistrates ex parte Darren Gratton* (25 November 1993) the magistrates had come to the conclusion that they could not consider attaching the applicant's liability to pay his community charge to his income support as a viable alternative to prison. Mr Justice MacPherson held that, in so concluding, the magistrates were "plainly wrong" and that, as such, there was a "fundamental flaw" in the case. In considering whether to order costs against the magistrates, he concluded:

> "I am wholly unable to find that there has been any perverse or outrageous conduct of any kind in this case. These are tricky cases. The law has been evolving in the last year or so."

He continued:

> "... Community charge liability should only be visited with prison (if I may use that shorthand expression) if there is no other way in which the money can be extracted. Prison is not to be used as a big stick or primarily as punishment but as a means of extracting the liability."

Mr Justice MacPherson stated that there may also have been a flaw in the case because the applicant was under 21 years of age at the time at which he was sentenced and the magistrates did not fulfil their requirement publicly to state that there was no alternative but prison in this case. However, he regarded it as unnecessary to conclude the case on that ground in the light of his earlier finding.

Lord Justice Kennedy stated in *R. v. Wolverhampton Magistrates' Court, ex parte Mould* [1992] RA 309:

> "...the power to commit to prison which is to be found in reg. 41 is plainly intended to be used as a weapon to extract payment rather than to punish......in the circumstances it might have been appropriate for the magistrate before making his order to ask the charging authority's representatives if any thought had been given to the possibility of an application to the Secretary of State [for deductions from income support]. I appreciate that ... a charging authority is not bound to take that course before seeking an order under reg. 41, but it would be relevant to the exercise of the magistrates' discretion to know if the possibility of [deductions] had at least been considered."

In *R. v. Newcastle-under-Lyme Justices, ex parte Massey* [1995] 1 All ER 120, Lord Justice Rose stated:

"A failure by justices to consider all possible alternative methods of enforcing payment before issuing a warrant for commitment might render their decision unreasonable in the Wednesbury sense ..."

In the unreported case of *R v. Middleton Magistrates ex parte Phillips* (29 October 1993) Mr Justice Potts stated:

"[A] court which finds a debtor guilty of wilful refusal to pay the relevant sum has a discretion. The court is not required to commit such a debtor to a term of imprisonment ... Before committing a debtor to prison, it is incumbent upon justices to consider all available alternatives to effect recovery of the sum due ...

It does not follow that, because the applicant had wilfully refused to pay the relevant sum, there was no alternative other than an immediate sentence of imprisonment. Regulation 41(3)(b) makes that plain ... The applicant had stated that she could pay off the arrears at £3 per week. This was a relevant factor for the justices' consideration in the exercise of the discretion conferred, in particular by Regulation 41(3)(b) ...

In my view the approach of the justices and the decision to commit this applicant to prison was in the circumstances fundamentally flawed."

Failure to pay fines

R. v. Norwich Magistrates' Court ex parte Lilly [1987] 151 JP 689 concerned an applicant who was committed to prison after having failed to pay two court-imposed fines. The Divisional Court held that a magistrates' court having inquired into an offender's means under section 82(3)(b) of the Magistrates'

Courts Act 1980 and satisfied itself that the default in payment was due to his wilful refusal or culpable neglect, was under a duty imposed by section 82(4)(b)(ii) to consider or try all other methods of enforcing payment before issuing a warrant of commitment. In the current case, it held that, on the evidence available, that duty had not been fulfilled and accordingly the application was granted and the two committal warrants were quashed.

During the course of his judgment, Mr Justice Farqu

harson stated as follows in relation to section 82(4)(b)(ii):

> "... The words of the subsection are peremptory. There is no discretion in the court, they have either to consider or try all the other methods of enforcing payment."

He continued:

> "... It needs to be emphasised that the proceedings which were taking place on September 9 before the Norwich Justices were not proceedings intended to punish the applicant. He had already been before the court for the offences that he had committed and the Justices on those occasions had decided that a fine was an appropriate sentence to pass.
>
> When the time came for enforcement, therefore, it was necessary for the Justices to go through the judicial exercise of seeing if there was any other method of enforcing payment of the fine, short of committing the applicant to prison, and that necessarily included a procedure whereby he was examined as to what property or other earnings or income he might have. It is not to be assumed merely on their experience of other cases by the Justices that the proceeding is a formality or unnecessary."

Persons under the age of 21

In *R. v. Newcastle Justices ex parte John Ashley* (12 October 1993), the fact that the applicant was under 21 at the time of his committal in respect of failure to pay community charge was accepted by the court to be the "major point" in the case. Mr Justice Laws, in quashing the committal order, concluded that the justices' decision to commit had been unlawful in that they had failed to have regard to their statutory responsibilities in the case under regulation 42(7) of the 1989 Regulations and Part I of the Criminal Justice Act 1982. He noted that the power to imprison a person under the age of 21 was only to be exercised if the court was of the opinion that no other method of dealing with him was appropriate and that it was the duty of the court, if of that opinion, to state in open court why the court believed that to be the case. He further noted that the magistrates had failed to state in open court why they believed that no alternative to imprisonment was available, that there was no evidence to show that the magistrates in fact felt that no other method was appropriate, or the reasons why they might so have felt; and that it was quite clear that alternatives to imprisonment had been available to them.

During the course of his judgment, Mr Justice Laws stated that the complaint made in respect of the decision to commit "went to an important aspect of the magistrates' court's jurisdiction under regulation 41 [of the 1989 Regulations]".

In *R. v. Oldham Justices and Another ex parte Cawley* [1997] Queen's Bench 1, each of three applicants, who were under 21 years of age, had defaulted in paying fines arising from summary criminal convictions and had been committed to prison. In each case the warrant of commitment was defective in failing to comply with the duty imposed by section 88(5) of the Magistrates' Courts Act 1980 to describe the justices' grounds for not placing an applicant of less than 21 years of age under supervision; and in failing to state the reason why no other method of dealing with such an applicant other than imprisonment was appropriate, contrary to section 1(5A) of the Criminal Justice Act 1982.

In the first two cases, the warrants also failed to specify upon what ground they were issued, contrary to section 82(6) of the Magistrates' Courts Act 1980 (which applied to both young and adult offenders). The Divisional Court held that a warrant of commitment which was defective for failure to comply with the requirements of sections 82(6) or 88(5) of the Magistrates' Courts Act 1980, or section 1(5A) of the Criminal Justice Act 1982, was not void, and detention under it was not unlawful, unless and until the warrant was quashed.

The nature of, and absence from, the hearing at which the warrant of commitment is issued

The cases below concern the situation where the applicant was present at the hearing inquiring into his means and circumstances and fixing a postponed sentence of imprisonment, but was absent from the subsequent hearing at which the warrant of commitment was issued (i.e. ordered to take effect, resulting in the immediate imposition of the previously postponed order of imprisonment).

In *R. v. Northampton Magistrates' Court ex parte Newell* [1992] RA 283 the Court of Appeal had to determine whether the magistrates were entitled under regulation 41 of the 1989 Regulations to issue a warrant of commitment against a charge payer who was absent from the final hearing at which the warrant was issued.

At first instance [1992] RA 190, 207, Mr Justice Henry held as follows:

"The power to issue a warrant arises after the court has inquired in the debtor's presence into whether his failure to pay which led to the liability order being made was due to his wilful refusal or culpable neglect *and* has found that it was. But they need not exercise that power immediately. They can, as here, fix the term of imprisonment and postpone the issue of the warrant on conditions. Section 12 [of the Interpretation Act 1978] then would entitle them to exercise that power (already vested in them) 'from time to time as the occasion requires' unless the contrary intention appears. The occasion certainly does not require a repeat of the [regulation] 41(2) inquiry. That is water under the bridge. The occasion does require application by the local authority, proper notice of that application to the defaulter to give him a fair opportunity to put his case as to why the warrant should not issue, followed by proof of a breach and notice and proper consideration of any relevant material put forward by the defaulter. That is all the occasion requires, and no contrary intention appears in the regulations. Therefore it seems to me... that natural justice requires notification to the applicant of that hearing."

The above conclusion was approved by the Master of the Rolls, Lord Donaldson, in the Court of Appeal.

Lord Justice Scott concluded as follows:

> "In this context, it goes without saying that it would be essential in, I would think, every case that the debtor be given proper notice of the time and place of the proposed application. If that were not done, the hearing would, I think, be fatally flawed. It is to be expected that, if the debtor were not present, the magistrates would not proceed with the hearing unless satisfied that proper notice of it had been given to the debtor. But if a debtor, having received proper notice, chooses not to attend the hearing, that is his affair, and for the magistrates to proceed in his absence cannot, in my opinion, possibly be represented as being in breach of the requirements of fairness or of natural justice."

In *R. v. Faversham and Sittingbourne Magistrates' Court ex parte Ursell* [1992] RA 99, Mr Justice Schiemann stated as follows in considering both the nature of the hearing at which the warrant of commitment was issued and the significance of the applicant not having notice of it:

"The magistrates in the present case appear to have accepted that a second hearing was necessary before the warrant of commitment was issued. They were right to do so. They did not apparently, however, consider that it was necessary for the debtor to have notice of the date and time of such a hearing. They clearly thought that she would have nothing new to say. They might well be right, but she is entitled, in my judgment, to be told of the date and time of the hearing as a matter of natural justice. The hearing affects her. It is held in public. She should have the right to be there. I do not, however, accept Mr

Emmerson's submission that the hearing cannot proceed if she chooses not to attend.

> The question arises: on what matter is a debtor entitled to address a court at such a hearing? Clearly she is entitled to put the authority to proof of non-payment. Further, in my judgment a debtor is entitled to draw the court's attention to any change of circumstances since the decision to fix a term of imprisonment which renders it inexpedient for the warrant of commitment to issue. There must, in my judgment, be an inherent power in the court to vary its own order in a case where, since the decision was made, the debtor has become incapable of earning, for instance by reason of an accident."

In *R. v. Hyndburn Justices ex parte Woolaghan* (2 December 1994) Mr Justice Jowitt held that, in the absence of sufficient proof of service of notice of the hearing at which the warrant of commitment was issued, the applicant was entitled to succeed on his application for judicial review. Mr Justice Jowitt stated as follows:

> "The difficulty, though, for the magistrates is, that when there is no appearance before them, they really have no way of telling whether this may be one of those, no doubt, not over frequent cases in which a letter has miscarried for one reason or another, perhaps because it has not been delivered or because the charge payer is absent for a continuing period from home, or because, in premises with a number of separate occupiers, a letter has got into the wrong hands. It seems, therefore, to follow that where there has been service by ordinary post, careful consideration would have to be given to the particular circumstances of the charge payer, before, if ever, concluding that the notice must have come into his hands."

In *R. v. Newcastle-upon-Tyne Justices ex parte Devine* [1998] RA 97, in which notice of the final hearing had been sent by the magistrates' court to the applicant's last known address, but was never received by the applicant as he had moved address and therefore did not appear at the hearing, Mr Justice Latham quoted the above-cited passage of Mr Justice Jowitt in *Woolaghan* and stated that the magistrates in the present case did not appear to have heeded it. This was notwithstanding that they had previously consented to an order being quashed because they had failed to carry out the appropriate inquiry to make sure that the notice of the final hearing must have come into the charge payer's hands. Mr Justice Latham referred to the fact that the magistrates knew that the applicant was intermittently unwell and therefore should also have enquired to ensure that the applicant was not suffering from one of his periodic illnesses at the time of the hearing. In all the circumstances he concluded that "the magistrates were quite wrong to issue a warrant of committal in his absence" and that their decision to do so was "vitiated".

In deciding to award costs against the justices, Mr Justice Latham cited and applied what he had said in a previous case in which magistrates had on two separate occasions fallen into the identical error of failing to make appropriate inquiry as to whether or not notice of the final hearing had been received by the applicant:

> "That seems to me to be behaviour which calls for strong disapproval, and because the principle which has apparently been ignored is one which involves the elementary step of ensuring that the person who is liable to lose his liberty has had an opportunity of knowing that the court was considering that particular course on that particular day, it is also a disregard for an elementary principle which every court ought to obey."

In *R. v. Doncaster Justices ex parte Hannan* (16 July 1998) (a case concerning the non-payment of a court-imposed fine, unlike the previous cases in this section which all concerned the non-payment of community charge) Lord Justice Rose in the Divisional Court held as follows:

> "[Counsel for the applicant] submits that to issue the Warrant for Commitment, with the knowledge which the Justices had [that she had not received notice of the hearing because that notice had been returned to the Justices marked "address inaccessible"] was an act of judicial impropriety and one which can properly be characterised as being perverse in that no reasonable bench of Justices would so have acted. (...)
>
> ... I am entirely satisfied that the submissions of [counsel for the applicant] advanced to this court are well-founded.
>
> This case illustrates how unwise it may be for Justices to make an order committing someone to prison when they do not know, because that person is not before them and because that person does not know of the date of the hearing, what the up-to-date circumstances are. It seems to me that, knowing that the applicant had not been served with notice of the proceedings, the Justices ought, much more prudently, to have adjourned the question of whether or not a Warrant of Commitment should be

issued until such time as she had been served with notice of the proceedings.

... I am satisfied that, in issuing the warrant in the circumstances in which they did, the Justices did act perversely..."

The case of *R. v. Doncaster Justices ex parte Christison and Jack* (13 May 1999), set out above under the heading "The circumstances of the cases", is also relevant in this context.

Awards of costs against the justices by the High Court

The applicable principles are set out in the above-cited *ex parte Christison and Jack* case (set out above under the heading "The circumstances of the cases").

Other issues

The length of the threat of imprisonment

In *R. v. Ealing Justices ex parte Cloves* [1991] RVR 169, the Divisional Court held that a committal order which had been suspended on the basis of the debtor paying £1 per week in the discharge of arrears of rates due was quashed since it would have taken over eight years for the debt to be discharged and the risk of committal removed. During the course of his judgment, Lord Justice Nolan stated as follows:

"... The criminal courts, when imposing fines upon convicted defendants of limited means, frequently provide for the fines to be paid by instalments over a period. There is no fixed limit to the period over which payment can be ordered. It has recently been indicated by the Court of Appeal that in appropriate circumstances a period of three years might not be excessive. (...)

... In my judgment it would be a very rare case indeed in which a defaulting rate- payer could properly be ordered, on pain of a sentence of imprisonment, to make payments in discharge of the arrears for a period anywhere near approaching eight years. In my judgment, with great respect to the Justices, unless they were confident that she could pay it off more quickly they should not have made the order in those terms."

In the above-cited case of *R. v. Newcastle-upon-Tyne Justices ex parte Devine,* Mr Justice Latham referred to the above-cited *ex parte Cloves* case in stating that the magistrates should not have imposed a suspended committal order which would have lasted for three and a half years. He was of the opinion that such an order should not be suspended for more than three years.

Mistakes on the face of the warrant

In *R. v. Erewash Borough Council and Ilkestone Justices ex parte Smedburg and Smedburg* [1994] RVR 60, the magistrates had issued committal warrants in respect of a failure to pay community charge, specifying in each case total arrears in payment of 378.58 pounds sterling (GBP), a sum different by a few pence from that in each of the applications for committal which were themselves incorrect, the correct amount being GBP 349.95.

Mr Justice Auld held that the magistrates should not have issued the committal warrants as a result of:

"... the incorrect figures in each of the applications for committal compounded by the fact that the sums specified in the warrants did not even correspond to those in the applications. It is vital in default proceedings of this sort, particularly those that may affect the liberty of the person against whom they are taken, that the alleged default is correctly specified and proved and that the default order is in the sum approved. See, e.g., per Lord Greene MR in *Gordon v. Gordon* [1946] 1 All ER 247, CA, at p 250."

The above was a reference to the following passage of the

***Gordon v. Gordon* case:**

"Attachment and committal are very technical matters, and as orders for committal or attachment affect the liberty of the subject such rules as exist in relation to them must be strictly obeyed. However disobedient the party against whom the order is directed may be, unless the process of committal and attachment has been carried out strictly in accordance with the rules he is entitled to his freedom."

The clerk to the justices

In *Practice Note (Justices' Clerks)* [1953] 1 Weekly Law Reports 1416, Lord Goddard CJ stated as follows:

> **"... if the clerk retires with the magistrates as a matter of course it is inevitable that the impression will be given that he may influence the justices as to the decision or sentence or both. A clerk should not retire with his justices as a matter of course, nor should they... merely [ask] him in every case to retire with them or [pretend] that they require his advice on a point of law. Subject to this, it is in the discretion of the justices to ask their clerk to retire with them if in any particular case it has become clear that they will need his advice."**

R v. the Governor of Brockhill Prison, ex parte Evans (No. 2)

In *R. v. the Governor of Brockhill Prison, ex parte Evans (No. 2)* [2000] 4 All England Reports 15, the House of Lords held that where the executive had detained a person unlawfully, that person was entitled to recover compensation for the tort of false imprisonment. In that case, the responsibility for calculating the date on which the respondent was to be released from prison lay with the Governor of the prison. He had calculated her date of release to be 18 November 1996. However, accepting her arguments on judicial review, the Divisional Court held that the release date should actually have been 17 September 1996. On appeal to the House of Lords, the Governor accepted that the respondent's continued detention after 17 September 1996 had therefore been unlawful. Nevertheless, he contended that he could not be liable for false imprisonment since he had complied with the law as it was understood at the time of his decision.

The House of Lords held that the tort of false imprisonment was one of strict liability and that its consequences could not be escaped even by showing that the Governor had acted in accordance with the view of the law which at the time was accepted by the court to be correct. There was no lawful justification for the action of the Governor, as the responsibility for calculating the release date lay with him, and not with the order of the court that sentenced the respondent to prison. The respondent was therefore entitled to compensation as it was agreed that her detention after 17 September 1996 was unlawful.

During the course of his judgment, Lord Hope stated that, as he had decided in her favour on other grounds, it was not necessary for the respondent to rely on her additional argument that the position of the Governor had been contrary to Article 5 of the Convention. However, he stated that as the issues that had arisen in the case had raised a novel point of law of some difficulty, it was of interest to see whether the provisions of Article 5 of the Convention supported the conclusion which he had determined to represent the present state of the domestic law. In the course of this consideration, Lord Hope stated the following:

> "The jurisprudence of the European Court of Human Rights indicates that there are various aspects to Art. 5(1) which must be satisfied in order to show that the detention is lawful for the purposes of that Article. The first question is whether the detention is lawful under domestic law. Any detention which is unlawful in domestic law will automatically be unlawful under Art. 5(1). It will thus give rise to an enforceable right to compensation under Art. 5(5), the provisions of which are not discretionary but mandatory."

A little later in his judgment, Lord Hope continued:

> "The question whether detention is or is not lawful under domestic law for the purposes of the Convention is a matter which the jurisprudence of the Strasbourg Court has left for decision by the domestic courts. The Divisional Court held that the respondent was entitled to release on 17 September 1996. It must follow that under domestic law her continued detention after that date was unlawful. This would indicate that there was a contravention of Art. 5(1)."

During the course of his judgment, Lord Hobhouse considered the arguments that the Solicitor General had presented on behalf of the Governor of the prison, and concluded as follows:

"The argument of the Solicitor General persistently confused a valid order for detention which is subsequently set aside with a valid order which is misinterpreted; it also confused a valid order which has not yet been set aside with an order which was never valid. These distinctions are basic to any legal system. An appeal against a conviction or sentence may lead to the conviction being quashed or the sentence being set aside or varied. But up to that time there were lawful orders of the sentencing court which were orders which had to be obeyed. (...)

The basic distinction between an ex facie invalid order and an order prima facie valid but which is liable to be set aside is also to be found in the Convention case-law as illustrated by *Benham v. the United Kingdom* (1996) 22 EHRR 293. The Commission had categorised the relevant order as coming into the former category and therefore held that there had been a breach of Art. 5; the Court disagreed, categorising the order for detention as prima facie valid, and held that there had been no breach of that Article. The Commission and the Court applied the same criteria in considering whether the detention had been lawful under the domestic law. Paragraph 42 of the judgment (at 320) relied on by the Solicitor General does not support his argument:

> 'A period of detention will in principle be lawful if it is carried out pursuant to a court order. A subsequent finding that the court erred under domestic law in making the order will not necessarily retrospectively affect the validity of the intervening period of detention. For this reason, the Strasbourg organs have consistently refused to uphold applications from persons convicted of criminal offences who complain that their convictions or sentences were found by the appellate courts to have been based on errors of facts or law.'

In the present case there was an order; it was never set aside nor did it have to be. The illegality arose because it did not authorise the detention which took place. The order was not obeyed."

The immunity of magistrates from civil proceedings

Magistrates enjoy a statutory immunity from civil liability in certain circumstances. Before the coming into force of section 108 of the Courts and Legal Services Act 1990 on 1 January 1991, this immunity was provided for by sections 44 and 45 of the Justices of the Peace Act 1979.

In brief, a magistrate was liable in damages for acts done by him in his official capacity if it could be proved either (1) that the act was done maliciously and without reasonable and probable cause, or (2) that it was performed outside or in excess of jurisdiction.

The position under section 108 of the Courts and Legal Services Act 1990 is now that an action lies against a magistrate only if it can be proved that he acted both in bad faith and in excess of jurisdiction.

Legal aid

Prior to 1 June 1997 neither the civil nor the criminal legal aid scheme provided for full representation before the magistrates in committal proceedings relating to the non-payment of a fine, community charge, council tax or non-domestic rates. The "Green Form" legal aid scheme provided two hours of help from a solicitor, and could include preparation for a court case, but did not provide for representation. The assistance by way of representation scheme ("ABWOR") enabled the court, in limited circumstances, to appoint a solicitor who happened to be within the court precincts to represent a party who would not otherwise be represented. The appointment might be made either of the court's own motion or on application by a solicitor. The court was under no obligation to advise a party of the possibility of such an appointment. The Duty Solicitor scheme, which provided representation for the accused in criminal cases before magistrates, did not extend to the proceedings with which this decision is concerned. Following the Court's judgment in the above-cited *Benham* case, where the Court found a breach of Article 6 §§ 1 and 3(c) of the Convention in respect of the applicant's complaint of a lack of legal representation, the United Kingdom enacted regulation 3(2) of the Legal Advice and Assistance (Scope) (Amendment) Regulations 1997 (S.I. 1997, No. 997). Under that provision, with effect from 1 June 1997, any person whose financial resources are such as to make him eligible is entitled to assistance by way of representation in proceedings before a magistrates' court in which he is likely to be "at risk of a term of imprisonment being fixed in his case (whether at the hearing for which ABWOR is granted or subsequently)" as a result of his failure to pay any sum which he has been ordered to pay.

COMPLAINTS

The applicants complained that their detention was unlawful and contrary to Article 5 § 1 of the Convention, and that, contrary to Article 5 § 5 of the Convention, they were not entitled to compensation therefor as, to be entitled to such compensation under domestic law, they would have had to have demonstrated that the magistrates had acted, *inter alia*, in bad faith.

The applicants further complained under Article 6 §§ 1 and 3(c) that they were not offered legal representation and were not represented at the hearing at which they were sentenced to a term of imprisonment. They affirmed their right to legal representation at a hearing at which their liberty was at stake. The only applicant who did not make this complaint expressly was Mackman (47143/99). In the context of these cases as a whole, the Court has decided, of its own motion, to examine her application under this head as well.

Some of the applicants originally complained under Article 6 § 1 that they had not had a hearing in the magistrates' court which was in compliance with the requirement of an independent and impartial tribunal in respect of certain of the actions of the clerk of the justices. However, in the light of the decision of the Court in *Mort v. the United Kingdom* (dec.), no. 44564/98, ECHR 2001-IX, the applicants decided not to pursue this complaint. In the light of the *Mort* decision, the Court does not see any reason to continue the examination of this complaint.

THE LAW

Preliminary submission that *Benham* and *Perks* were wrongly decided

The parties' submissions

The applicants

It was submitted on behalf of all of the applicants, except two, that the above-cited cases of *Benham* and *Perks* were wrongly determined. It was submitted that the Court was not directed to all the appropriate domestic jurisprudence when it considered the *Benham* case. As a result it was submitted that the Court established an artificial and erroneous distinction between decisions to detain which were "within" and those which were "outside" the jurisdiction of the competent committing tribunal.

It was further submitted that, in any event, the essential principle of domestic law had recently been clarified in the above-cited passage of Lord Hope in *R. v. the Governor of Brockhill Prison ex parte Evans* (No. 2) [2000] 4 All England Reports 15 that: "Any detention which is unlawful in domestic law will automatically be unlawful under Article 5(1). It will thus give rise to an enforceable right to compensation under Article 5(5), the provisions of which are not discretionary but mandatory."

This was averred by the applicants to be "the correct approach in domestic law".

The applicants submitted that the distinction between decisions made “inside jurisdiction” and “outside jurisdiction” created two classes of unlawfulness which was in itself contrary to the necessity for clarity in the law and left the dividing line between those two classes of unlawfulness unclear. The applicants submitted that it was appropriate for this issue to be reconsidered by the Court as it gave rise to a matter of considerable importance to the present applicants and many others.

The observations submitted on behalf of the applicant Wood (30395/96) elaborated upon this point further. It was submitted that the acceptance by the representative of Mr Benham, as reflected at paragraph 43 of the *Benham* judgment, that there existed in English law a distinction between acts outside and those within the jurisdiction of the justices was wrong. The applicant submitted that since 1969 that distinction had been removed. Without citing any particular passage therefrom, the applicant referred to the above-cited *Anisminic* case in relation to this submission.This applicant further submitted that the matter was confused in *Benham* by the above-cited *McC v. Mullan* case in which the distinction between acts outside and inside jurisdiction came into play by virtue of section 15 of the Northern Ireland Act 1964, which provided that no action for damages should succeed against magistrates unless the court was satisfied that the magistrate acted without or in excess of jurisdiction. It was submitted that that distinction was not one that was established in English law. Accordingly it was submitted that the Court was wrong to proceed on that basis.

The applicant then reiterated the arguments set out above that were raised in respect of all applicants that *Benham* was wrongly decided and that the correct approach of English law was as set out above by Lord Hope in the *Evans* case as set out above.

The applicant G.M. (34341/96) further submitted that the passage of the speech of Lord Hobhouse in *Evans* set out above and relied upon by the Government was merely a citation by His Lordship of the legal background for the purposes of the *Evans* case. It was averred that the passage concerned was not determinative of Lord Hobhouse’s judgment and, in any event, did not form a part of the reasoning of any of the other judges in that case.

he Government

The Government did not accept that the *Evans* decision cast doubt upon the conclusions of the Court in *Benham* and *Perks*. The

Government argued that in the *Evans* case the House of Lords was concerned with detention by the prison authorities. The question was whether those authorities had detained Ms Evans longer than was permitted by the court order under which she had been committed to prison. The validity of that court order was not in doubt. Therefore, the Government contended that the House of Lords did not have to consider the distinction in English law between a court order which was within the jurisdiction of the court making it, and one which was made in excess of jurisdiction. The *Evans* decision had, submitted the Government, to be read in that context. In any event, the Government submitted that that part of Lord Hope's speech cited by the applicants was entirely consistent with paragraph 41 of the judgment of the Court in *Benham*.

The Government further submitted that in the judgment of Lord Hobhouse there was a clear endorsement of precisely the distinction recognised in *Benham.* They relied on the above-cited passage of Lord Hobhouse's judgment in which he stated that:

The basic distinction between an ex facie invalid order and an order prima facie valid but which is liable to be set aside is also to be found in the Convention case-law as illustrated by *Benham v. the United Kingdom*...

> The Commission had categorised the relevant order as coming into the former category and therefore held that there had been a breach of Art. 5; the Court disagreed, categorising the order for detention as prima facie valid, and held that there had been no breach of that Article. The Commission and the Court applied the same criteria in considering whether the detention had been lawful under the domestic law."

The Government submitted that the Court had no reason to reconsider its conclusions in *Benham* or *Perks* because of the decision in the *Evans* case.

The Court's assessment

The Court recalls the following general principles that were stated at paragraphs 39-44 of the above-cited *Benham* judgment, and reiterated, in large part, at paragraph 62 of the *Perks* judgment:

"39. The Court first observes that this case falls to be examined under sub- paragraph (b) of Article 5 para. 1, since the purpose of the detention was to secure the fulfilment of Mr Benham's obligation to pay the community charge owed by him.

The main issue to be determined in the present case is whether the disputed detention was 'lawful', including whether it complied with 'a procedure prescribed by law'. The Convention here essentially refers back to national law and states the obligation to conform to the substantive and procedural rules thereof, but it requires in addition that any deprivation of liberty should be consistent with the purpose of Article 5, namely to protect individuals from arbitrariness....

It is in the first place for the national authorities, notably the courts, to interpret and apply domestic law. However, since under Article 5 § 1 failure to comply with domestic law entails a breach of the Convention, it follows that the Court can and should exercise a certain power to review whether this law has been complied with. A period of detention will in principle be lawful if it is carried out pursuant to a court order. A subsequent finding that the court erred under domestic law in making the order will not necessarily retrospectively affect the validity of the intervening period of detention.

For this reason, the Strasbourg organs have consistently refused to uphold applications from persons convicted of criminal offences who complain that their convictions or sentences were found by the appellate courts to have been based on errors of fact or law.

It was agreed by those appearing before the Court that the principles of English law which should be taken into account in this case distinguished between acts of a magistrates' court which were within its jurisdiction and those which are in excess of jurisdiction. The former were valid and effective unless or until they were overturned by a superior court, whereas the latter were null and void from the outset.

It was further submitted that the appropriate test under English law for deciding whether or not magistrates acted within their jurisdiction was that laid down by the House of Lords in *McC. v. Mullan* ... The third limb of that test was relevant to the instant case, namely that magistrates exceeded their jurisdiction when they made an order which had no foundation in law because of a failure to observe a statutory condition precedent.

This limb was applied by the Court of Appeal in *Manchester City Magistrates' Court, ex parte Davies* ... In that case the appeal court found that magistrates had acted in excess of jurisdiction when they committed a man to prison for non-payment of rates without having carried out the inquiry required by law as to whether his failure to pay was due to culpable neglect.

> In each of the two cases referred to above it was necessary for the courts to decide the jurisdictional issue, because at the relevant time damages could be awarded against magistrates who acted in excess of jurisdiction. However, section 108 of the Courts and Legal Services Act 1990 has since changed the law to provide that there is no right to damages unless magistrates acted in bad faith... For this reason, when the Divisional Court reviewed the magistrates' order for Mr Benham's detention, there was no reason under English law for it to decide whether or not the order had been made in excess of jurisdiction."

The Court has considered the applicants' arguments that the cases of *Benham* and *Perks* were wrongly decided on the basis that the distinction drawn between decisions to detain which were within and outside the jurisdiction of the sentencing tribunal was artificial and erroneous; and that the essential principle of domestic law had recently been clarified by Lord Hope in the above-cited case of *Evans*.

However, the Court does not regard the *Evans* case as being capable of casting doubt upon the statement of the law as set out in the above-cited *Benham* and *Perks* judgments. The Court recalls that in *Evans* the validity of the order of the court sentencing the respondent to prison was not in doubt.

> he House of Lords did not, therefore, have to determine the case on the basis of the distinction between a court order which had been made within jurisdiction and one which had been made in excess of jurisdiction. The issue in *Evans* was whether the Governor of the prison in which the respondent was kept had correctly calculated the date upon which she was to be released. The Divisional Court held that the Governor had not calculated the date of release correctly and had, as a result, detained the respondent for 59 days beyond the date on which she should have been released. It was agreed by the parties in the House of Lords that her detention for those 59 days, which arose solely out of the Governor's error in calculating her release date, had therefore been unlawful.
>
> The Court also does not find the above-cited passage of Lord Hope in *Evans*, relied upon by the applicants, to be of assistance to them. As can be seen from the words of Lord Hope himself, that passage does no more than restate the jurisprudence of this Court that any detention which is unlawful in domestic law will automatically

be unlawful under Article 5 § 1 of the Convention. It was precisely the issue of whether the detention was unlawful under domestic law that was under consideration in both *Benham* and *Perks*. For that reason, the Court re-iterated the principles of its own case-law at paragraph 42 of the *Benham* judgment, cited above, including the general rule that a period of detention would in principle be lawful if it was carried out pursuant to a court order.

Indeed, far from challenging that statement of the law, the Court notes that in *Evans* Lord Hobhouse specifically referred to it. He pointed out that the distinction to which he had alluded between an *ex facie* invalid order and an order *prima facie* valid but which was liable to be set aside was not only "basic to any legal system", but had also been specifically recognised by this Court in the *Benham* case. Lord Hobhouse proceeded to quote paragraph 42 of the Court's judgment in *Benham* in full. Neither Lord Hobhouse, nor any other Law Lord, made any criticism of the approach adopted by this Court in *Benham*.

The applicants have also failed to persuade the Court that the distinction between acts within and acts outside the jurisdiction was removed by the *Anisminic* case.

The Court notes that the applicants, in making this submission, did not refer to any particular passage of *Anisminic*, nor to any other domestic case-law.

Moreover, and in any event, the Court regards as significant that the House of Lords in the subsequent above-cited case of *McC v. Mullan* held that the question to be determined in that case was whether the magistrates had acted within or outside their jurisdiction. The Court recalls that in addressing that question Lord Bridge specifically referred to *Anisminic* and stated that he did not believe that what he termed "the novel test of excess of jurisdiction which emerges from the *Anisminic* case" in the context of the supervisory jurisdiction of superior courts over inferior tribunals, to have "any application whatever" to the question of whether the magistrates had acted without or in excess of jurisdiction in the *McC* case.

Similarly, the Court notes that the Court of Appeal in the above-cited case of *R. v. Manchester City Magistrates' Court, ex parte Davies* also considered the *Anisminic* case and concluded that it was plain that, in the context of whether a magistrate had acted without or in excess of jurisdiction, the word "jurisdiction" had a wider meaning than that given to it by Lord Reid in *Anisminic*.

It is therefore clear to the Court that neither the House of Lords in *McC* nor the Court of Appeal in *Davies* understood the *Anisminic* case to have abolished the distinction between acts within and acts outside jurisdiction. Indeed, the *McC* and *Davies* cases dealt specifically with the question of whether the acts of the magistrates were within or outside their jurisdiction; and those cases were decided after the decision of, and with specific reference to, the House of Lords in *Anisminic*.

Furthermore, the Court notes that the Court of Appeal in *Davies* specifically pointed out that the relevant legislation in Northern Ireland was the same as the relevant legislation in England (see section 3 of the heading "Relevant domestic law" above). The Court further notes that the *Davies* case was decided under English law. The Court is therefore not convinced by the apparent suggestion of the applicant Wood (no. 30395/96) that the distinction between acts within and acts outside the jurisdiction came into play by virtue of section 15 of the Northern Ireland Act 1964, and that that distinction was not one that was established in English law.

The Court recalls that its judgments both in *Benham* and *Perks* followed an oral hearing at which each side was represented. The principles of English law to be applied were agreed between the parties.

Those principles are set out under section 3 of the heading "Relevant domestic law" above. For the reasons expressed, the Court does not find that either *Anisminic* or *Evans* cast doubt upon the validity of the relevant domestic law set out in the *Perks* and *Benham* judgments. The Court therefore rejects the applicants' submissions that those cases were wrongly decided and that the principles of law stated therein should now be reconsidered by the Court. The Court shall therefore proceed to consider the admissibility of the present applications in line with its previous case-law.

<u>Article 5</u>

The applicants complained that their detention was unlawful and contrary to Article 5 § 1 of the Convention, and that, contrary to Article 5 § 5 of the Convention, they were not entitled to compensation therefor under domestic law.

Article 5 reads, insofar as relevant, as follows:

Article 5 - Right to liberty and security

"1. Everyone has the right to liberty and security of person. No one shall be deprived of his liberty save in the following cases and in accordance with a procedure prescribed by law:

The lawful arrest or detention of a person for non-compliance with the lawful order of a court or in order to secure the fulfillment of any obligation prescribed by law;

5. Everyone who has been the victim of arrest or detention in contravention of the provisions of this article shall have an enforceable right to compensation."

The parties' submissions

The Government

The Government submitted that the same principal considerations were relevant to the present applications as were examined by the Court in the *Benham* judgment at paragraphs 35-47 and in the *Perks* judgment at paragraphs 62-74.]

They contended that in the present applications all but one of the complaints under Article 5 raised one or more of three principal arguments:
(i) that there was no adequate means inquiry, in the sense that additional evidence could have been demanded and was not or that alternatives to imprisonment were not adequately explored, or that the conclusion reached was not consistent with the evidence in fact adduced; (ii) that there was no further means inquiry where the issue of the warrant of commitment had been postponed on conditions before it was in fact issued; and (iii) that the defaulter was not before the magistrates' court on the occasion on which a postponed warrant of commitment was issued.

The Government submitted that the first and second of the above issues were considered explicitly by the Court in the *Perks* judgment, at paragraphs 62-70. The Government pointed out that on that occasion the Court found that it could not be said that the orders in question were not within the jurisdiction of the magistrates' courts by which they were made.

The Government submitted that, in relation to the third issue, the High Court judgments cited in the relevant consent orders established that in some circumstances the committal of a defaulter in his or her absence would be an unreasonable exercise of the magistrates' discretion. The Government contended that those domestic judgments did not establish that the magistrates had no jurisdiction to make such orders in those circumstances.

The Government drew the Court's attention to the fact that one of the applicants in the *Perks* case, Mr Beattie, had himself been absent when the postponed warrant was issued in his case, but that nevertheless he had not pursued his complaint under Article 5 in front of the Court (see paragraphs 31-34 of the *Perks* judgment). The Government further pointed out that in each of the present cases the applicant was present before the magistrates' court when the means inquiry was held In all bar one case [Parker (46416/99)] the Government submitted that there was no indication, whether in the order of the High Court or elsewhere, that the magistrates failed to observe an express statutory condition precedent or made any other error such as to render their decision to commit the applicant in excess of their jurisdiction.

They contended that in the present applications all but one of the complaints under Article 5 raised one or more of three principal arguments:
(i) that there was no adequate means inquiry, in the sense that additional evidence could have been demanded and was not or that alternatives to imprisonment were not adequately explored, or that the conclusion reached was not consistent with the evidence in fact adduced; (ii) that there was no further means inquiry where the issue of the warrant of commitment had been postponed on conditions before it was in fact issued; and (iii) that the defaulter was not before the magistrates' court on the occasion on which a postponed warrant of commitment was issued.

The Government submitted that the first and second of the above issues were considered explicitly by the Court in the *Perks* judgment, at paragraphs 62-70. The Government pointed out that on that occasion the Court found that it could not be said that the orders in question were not within the jurisdiction of the magistrates' courts by which they were made.

The Government submitted that, in relation to the third issue, the High Court judgments cited in the relevant consent orders established that in some circumstances the committal of a defaulter in his or her absence would be an unreasonable exercise of the magistrates' discretion. The Government contended that those domestic judgments did not establish that the magistrates had no jurisdiction to make such orders in those circumstances.

The Government drew the Court's attention to the fact that one of the applicants in the *Perks* case, Mr Beattie, had himself been absent when the postponed warrant was issued in his case, but that nevertheless he had not pursued his complaint under Article 5 in front of the Court (see paragraphs 31-34 of the *Perks* judgment). The Government further pointed out that in each of the present cases the applicant was present before the magistrates' court when the means inquiry was held In all bar one case [Parker (46416/99)] the Government submitted that there was no indication, whether in the order of the High Court or elsewhere, that the magistrates failed to observe an express statutory condition precedent or made any other error such as to render their decision to commit the applicant in excess of their jurisdiction.

In those circumstances, the Government contended that it could not be concluded that the magistrates had acted in excess of jurisdiction in any of those cases. Therefore, the Government submitted that there had not been any violation of Article 5 in those cases.

The Government disputed the applicants' contention that the present applications were indistinguishable from the decisions of the Commission in the cases of *Johnson v. the United Kingdom* (no. 28455/95), *Poole v. the United Kingdom* (no. 28190/95) and *S.D. v. the United Kingdom* (no. 25283/94) (Commission reports of 9 September 1998). They submitted that in *S.D.* and *Johnson* the High Court had delivered judgments in which the committals to prison were held to be invalid; and that in *Poole* the consent order had in terms recited a failure to observe a statutory condition precedent.

The Government interpreted the applicants' reference to the domestic case of *R. v. Nottingham Justices ex parte Hollingsworth* (4 June 1997) (see below) as a suggestion that the High Court orders were silent about whether their committals were in excess of jurisdiction because it was unnecessary for the High Court to decide that question for English legal purposes. The Government acknowledged that the Court was competent to investigate whether the committals of the applicants had taken place in excess of jurisdiction, as it had done in its *Benham* and *Perks* judgments. However, the Government pointed out that in almost all of the present applications the proceedings in the High Court had been determined by a consent order.

The terms of the order were usually prepared by the applicant's legal advisers and the parties were free to choose upon what basis such an order was expressed to be made.

The Government therefore submitted that where the consent order did not record that the order for detention had been made "in excess of jurisdiction" or "without satisfying a statutory condition precedent" the Court could infer that no basis for such a statement was perceived at that time.

In the remaining case of Parker (46416/99), the Government noted that the High Court had ruled that the magistrates had lacked all power to issue a warrant of commitment in the circumstances of that case. In those circumstances, the Government accepted that, in that application, it could be concluded that the magistrates had acted in excess of jurisdiction and, therefore, in violation of Article 5.

The applicants

Kenneth WOOD (30395/96)

The applicant noted that the consent order in his case was made on the basis that the justices had acted unreasonably in having failed to have regard to the change in his circumstances; and that in the *Perks* case the Court had concluded that a further inquiry into the applicant's circumstances was not a statutory condition precedent and that the magistrates had therefore not exceeded their jurisdiction. The applicant in the present case did not explicitly submit that the consent order made demonstrated that the magistrates had acted in excess of jurisdiction. Instead he submitted that the cases of *Benham* and *Perks* were wrongly decided (for the reasons set out above) and that his application should be determined in accordance with the above-cited passage of Lord Hope in the *Evans* case. He concluded that there had therefore been a breach of Article 5.

Robert WALLER (34327/96)

In the light of the *Perks* judgment, the applicant did not pursue his complaint under Article 5 §§ 1 and 5 of the Convention. He accepted that the decisions of the magistrates in his case were not outside their jurisdiction even though they may have been wrong in law.

G.M. (34341/96)

The applicant maintained that the magistrates had acted in excess of jurisdiction in committing him to prison. Referring to the heads set out in the consent order, he submitted as follows:

Head (a): The applicant submitted that the justices could not have been properly satisfied to the requisite standard of proof that the applicant had both wilfully refused and culpably neglected to pay the sums due. He referred to the letter from his solicitor dated 30 June 1995, which it was undisputed was read out to the justices at the hearing. That letter set out in some detail the applicant's income and expenditure. It also set out details of his personal circumstances. The applicant submitted that the justices were informed, in that letter, that the applicant had sought the assistance of the Money Advice Worker of his District Council on 7 February 1995, that he had every intention of honouring his debts and that he had contacted the Department of Social Security with a view to his arrears being deducted directly from his income support.

The applicant referred to the case of *R. v. South Tyneside Justices ex parte Stuart Martin* to submit that any finding of either wilful refusal or culpable neglect had to be made to the criminal standard of proof and that, on the evidence before them, the justices could not properly have made any such finding. The applicant further submitted that that finding was, in the light of the letter of 30 June 1995, so perverse as to render it a gross and obvious irregularity of procedure within the meaning of the *McC* case.

Head (b): The applicant submitted that the justices failed to have regard to the purpose of imprisonment in his case. He referred to the above-cited cases of *ex parte Mould* and *ex parte Gratton* to submit that the purpose of imprisonment was primarily to coerce payment rather than to punish and that it was therefore incumbent upon the justices to consider all the alternatives of gathering the outstanding debt before committing the applicant to prison. He further submitted that there were a number of alternatives in his case that the justices could have used and that his case was not an exceptional one which required that he should be sent to prison. The applicant emphasised that he was committed to prison at his first hearing before the magistrates. In all the circumstances, he argued that his committal on that occasion amounted to a gross and obvious irregularity of procedure.

Head (c): The applicant accepted that justices were not normally required to give reasons for their decisions. However, the applicant submitted that was because there was ordinarily a right of appeal to the Crown Court against their decisions (which did not exist in community charge cases) and because there was generally a right to require the justices to state a case to the High Court on any question of law.

The applicant referred to the case of *R. v. Poole Justices ex parte Benham* [1991] RVR 217 to submit that the remedy of appealing by way of case stated was an ineffective one in community charge cases. In those circumstances, he submitted by reference to the domestic case of *R v. Higher Education Funding Council ex parte Institute of Dental Surgery* [1994] 1 WLR 242 (Queen's Bench Division), that there were circumstances in which the common law required reasons to be given for certain decisions, which should be applied to his case.

The *Institute of Dental Surgery* case considered whether academic judgments were in a class of case for which the decision required reasons to be given and held that they were not.

The applicant relied upon the summary given by Mr Justice Sedley in that case as to the circumstances in which a court should give reasons to submit that reasons should have been given in his case. Mr Justice Sedley held that there was no general duty to give reasons for a decision, but that there were classes of case where there was such a duty. One such class was where the subject matter was an interest so highly regarded by the law (for example, personal liberty), that fairness required that reasons, at least for particular decisions, be given as of right. Another such class was where the decision appeared aberrant.

Head (d): The applicant submitted that the error of the justices in issuing the committal warrant for the wrong amount was such an elementary error that it clearly took the decision outside their jurisdiction. It was, submitted the applicant, a gross and obvious irregularity of procedure. The applicant referred to the domestic case of *ex parte Smedburg and Smedburg*, referred to under the heading "Relevant domestic law" above.

The applicant pointed out that it was clear from the face of the consent order that the magistrates in his case agreed to bear the costs of his application for judicial review. He referred to the test applied by the domestic courts in deciding whether it was appropriate for magistrates to bear a defendant's costs (see "Relevant domestic law" above). The applicant submitted that the test applied for the award of costs against magistrates was analogous to the test applied as to whether a decision fell outside the magistrates' jurisdiction. The applicant argued that the magistrates, in agreeing to pay his costs, recognised the fundamental nature of the errors that they made.

The applicant submitted that, whether taken individually or together, each of the above matters rendered the decision of the magistrates to commit him to prison one that was in breach of Article 5 of the Convention.

Anthony TOWNSEND (42039/98)

The applicant referred to the terms of the consent order that was made in his case. He submitted that the decision in the domestic case of *ex parte Newell* made clear that magistrates were obliged to satisfy themselves that he had been served with notice of the hearing before they could proceed with that hearing. He submitted that such an obligation amounted to a condition precedent.

He further submitted that his detention was not lawful as a proper means inquiry and a finding of culpable neglect were conditions precedent to the issue of a committal warrant. Neither was present in his case. Nor could the justices have been satisfied to the requisite standard of proof that he had culpably neglected to have paid the sums that were due.

The applicant further submitted that his detention had been arbitrary and therefore in contravention of Article 5 of the Convention. He contended that his case was very similar to the above-cited previous Convention cases of *Johnson v. the United Kingdom*, *Poole v. the United Kingdom* and *S.D. v. the United Kingdom*. He further noted the apparent failure of the Government to give any meaningful consideration to the facts of his case and their failure to recognise the concessions that they had made in the cases of *Johnson, Poole* and *S.D.*

Mark WOOD (47441/99)

The applicant maintained that, for the reasons set out in the consent order of the High Court, his detention had been unlawful within domestic law and was neither in accordance with a procedure prescribed by law nor lawful within the meaning of Article 5 § 1 of the Convention. He contended that his case was very similar to the cases of *Johnson*, *Poole* and *S.D* (referred to above). He argued that it was the failure by the magistrates to conduct the inquiries required by law which took their decisions beyond their jurisdiction. He noted the apparent failure of the Government to give any meaningful consideration to the facts of his case, as well as their failure to recognise the concessions that they had made in the cases of *Johnson, Poole* and *S.D.*

The remaining applicants

Composite submissions were made on behalf of the remaining applicants. In relation to Parker (46416/99) it was submitted on her behalf that it had been agreed by all parties that her detention constituted a breach of Article 5 §§ 1 and 5.

In relation to the remaining applicants it was submitted as follows:

The grounds upon which the High Court quashed the decisions of the magistrates

The applicants submitted that the grounds upon which the High Court made a determination in a particular case were not determinative as to the totality of the unlawfulness in that case. Referring to the domestic case of *R.*
v. Nottingham Justices ex parte Hollingsworth (4 June 1997), the applicants pointed out that the discretionary powers of the High Court could not be used solely for the purposes of facilitating a collateral application for just satisfaction under the Convention. They contended that where a matter had been resolved by other means, no further cause of action lay before the High Court in order to determine whether the initial decision of the tribunal to detain the applicant was lawful or otherwise. The applicant submitted that the Court should therefore consider the merits of those challenges which had not been determined by the High Court because that court had determined the matter on other grounds.

Failure to undertake an appropriate means inquiry

The applicants stated that the Government had accepted that the magistrates had acted outside their jurisdiction and duly agreed settlements in the cases of *S.D.*, *Poole* and *Johnson* (referred to above). The applicants referred to the requirements of regulation 41(2) of the 1989 Regulations and to section 82(4) of the Magistrates' Courts Act 1980. They further submitted that the requirements for an appropriate inquiry in relation to a finding of wilful refusal and/or culpable neglect had been well established in a number of domestic cases. They referred to the above-cited cases of *R. v. Manchester City Magistrates' Court ex parte Davies*, *R v. Stafford Justices ex parte Johnson*, *R. v. South Tyneside Justices ex parte Martin*, *R. v. Woking Justices ex parte Johnstone* and *DPP v. Meara*.

The applicants submitted that a failure to undertake an appropriate inquiry, or to follow the conditions precedent set out in the above statutory provisions, would render the determination of the magistrates outside their jurisdiction and therefore in breach of Article 5 § 1. **The applicants further referred to the above-cited domestic case of *R. v. Leeds City Justices ex parte Kennett* to submit that it was a condition precedent for the magistrates to inquire into the circumstances of an applicant at the time at which each liability order was made.**

The applicants submitted that in each of the following cases the magistrates failed to make appropriate inquiry into the applicants' means and circumstances and/or that the finding that the applicants had wilfully refused or culpably neglected to pay was unsustainable. They contended that the determination in each case was in breach of Article 5 § 1 and that none of the following applications could be distinguished from the cases of *S.D.*, *Poole* and *Johnson*: Hughes (36267/97), Kershaw-Field (36367/97), Kane (37706/97), Edwards (38260/97), Hagyard (39378/97), Garnham (41593/98), Hartley (42097/98), Sheppard (45420/99), Swaine (45844/99), Strickland (46140/99), Jones (46326/99), Mackman (47143/99), Watts (2490/03), Jelley (54969/00), Merry (54973/00), Taylor (56231/00), Reilly (56232/00) and Christison (56429/00).

(c) **Other unlawful committal**

The applicants submitted that, in addition to making a finding as to the adequacy of the inquiry into the applicants' means and/or circumstances, the High Court had quashed the determination of the magistrates on the grounds that they had acted unlawfully in committing the applicant to prison (i) in their absence and (ii) when there had been alternative methods of enforcement available to them, in a number of cases contrary to the requirements of Part I of the Criminal Justice Act 1982. The applicants repeated their submission that the Court should reconsider its judgment in the *Benham* case for the reasons set out above.

The applicants presented their arguments in tabular form. They submitted that the table showed cases in which findings or uncontested submissions had either been accepted, or not refuted, by the High Court. They contended that in those circumstances the decision to commit the applicant to prison should be considered to be contrary to Article 5 § 1. The Court has reproduced the applicants' tabular submissions.

Name (application no.)	CC or F[1]	Inadequate Means Inquiry	Committal in absence	Alternative enforcement
Sanders (35445/97)	F	N/k[2]	No[3]	Yes[4]
Hughes (36267/97)	CC	Yes - Martin, Kennett[5]	No	N/k
Kershaw-Field (36367/97)	CC	Yes - Martin	Yes	N/k
Barker (37551/97)	CC	N/k	Yes - Woolaghan	N/k
Kane (37706/97)	CC	Yes - Martin	Yes - Woolaghan	N/a[6]
Edwards (38260/97)	CC	Yes - Martin	Yes	N/a
Massey (38261/97)	CC	N/k	Yes - Woolaghan	N/a
Hagyard (39378/97)	CC	Yes - Martin	Yes - Woolaghan	N/k
Crilly (41590/98)	F	N/k	No	N/k
Garnham (41593/98)	CC	Yes - Kennett, Martin	Yes	N/k
Ellis (42040/98)	F	N/k	Yes - Recorded delivery letter returned[7]	Yes - U 21[8]
Hartley (42097/98)	F	Yes	No	Yes
Sheppard (45420/99)	CC	Yes - Kennett, Martin	Yes	N/k
Swaine (45844/99)	F	Yes	No	Yes
Strickland (46140/99)	CC	Yes - Kennett	No	N/k
Jones (46326/99)	CC	Yes - Martin	Yes - Woolaghan	N/k
Mackman (47143/99)	CC	Yes - Kennett	N/k	N/k
Mason (47144/99)	F	N/k	Yes - Hannan	N/k
Houghton (47985/99)	CC	N/k	Yes - aware of incapacity[9]	N/k
Watts (53062/99)	F	N/k	Yes - Hannan	N/k
Watts (2490/03)	CC	Yes - Cox	Yes - Hannan	Yes
Middleton (2483/03)	F	N/k	Yes	Yes - Lilly
Shelley (2484/03)	F	N/k	Yes	Yes - Lilly
Pitt (53111/99)	F	N/k	Yes	Yes - Lilly
Slater (2460/03)	F	N/k	No	Yes - U 21
Fletcher (2482/03)	F	N/k	No	Yes - Lilly
Jelley (54969/00)	F	Yes	Yes	Yes
Merry (54973/00)	F	Yes	Yes - Christison & Jack	N/a
Watson (54997/00)	F	N/k	No	Yes - Lilly
Armstrong (55046/00)	F	N/k	Yes	Yes - Lilly
Jackson (55068/00)	F	N/k	Yes - Hannan	N/k
Taylor (55071/00)	F	N/k	Yes	Yes - Lilly
Donald (56109/00)	F	N/a	Yes - Hannan	N/a
Taylor (56231/00)	F	Yes - Johnson	Yes	N/k

Name (application no.)	CC or F[1]	Inadequate Means Inquiry	Committal in absence	Alternative enforcement
Reilly (56232/00)	CC	Yes - Martin	Yes - Christison & Jack	N/a
Condon (56233/00)	F	N/k	Yes	Yes
Christison (56429/00)	CC	Yes	Yes - Hannan	N/a
Wilson (56441/00)	F	N/k	Yes - Hannan	N/k

1 This column sets out whether the arrears arose in relation to community charge ("CC") or fines ("F") cases.

2 The letters "N/k" represent situations where the applicants submitted that no conclusion could be drawn as to whether the High Court accepted their submission in relation to this issue.

3 The word "No" signified that the applicant's submission in respect of this issue had been rejected by the High Court; or, in relation to the fourth column of the table, that the applicant had been present at the committal hearing.

4 The word "Yes" signified that the applicant's submission that the magistrates had failed to undertake an appropriate means inquiry or had failed to adopt alternative enforcement proceedings had been accepted or had not been refuted. In relation to the fourth column, it signified that the applicant had been committed to prison in his/her absence.

5 The word "Yes" followed by a name was submitted to signify that the High Court had, respectively, made a specific finding that the magistrates had failed to undertake an adequate means inquiry, or that their decision to commit the applicant to prison in his/her absence was unlawful, or that they had failed properly to consider the alternatives to the issue of a committal warrant. The name following the word "Yes" represented the abbreviated name of the case which the applicants submitted contained the test that should have been applied in the circumstances. (The name in the table corresponds to the final word in the title of the relevant domestic case cited in full in the section headed "Relevant domestic law" above.)

6 The letters "N/a" were submitted to signify a situation in which the applicant was not required to pursue this ground of challenge as a result of the magistrates' decision having been quashed on an alternative ground.

7 The words "Yes-recorded delivery letter returned" was submitted to signify that the High Court had made a specific finding that the decision of the magistrates to commit the applicant to prison in his absence was unlawful, in part because of the imputed knowledge of

the magistrates that the applicant had not received notice of the hearing.

8 The phrase "Yes-U21" was submitted to signify that the magistrates had failed to fulfil the requirements of Part I of the Criminal Justice Act 1982.

9 The phrase "Yes-aware of incapacity" was submitted to signify that the High Court had made a specific finding that the decision of the magistrates to commit the applicant to prison in her absence had been unlawful in part because of the imputed knowledge of the magistrates that the applicant was incapacitated and unable to attend the hearing.

The Court's assessment

The grounds upon which the High Court quashed the decisions of the magistrates

In so far as the submission of the applicants based upon their reference to the case of *R. v. Nottingham Justices ex parte Hollingsworth* was intended to invite the Court to consider grounds that do not appear on the face of the consent orders or within the body of the judgments of the High Court, the Court rejects that submission. The Court notes that the grounds were contained either within an order that was made by consent or within a judgment that was delivered following oral argument. In those circumstances the applicants were entitled to raise any grounds upon which they wished to rely in the High Court proceedings. The Court further notes that the applicants have failed to provide any detailed submissions about what further grounds, if any, they consider should be taken into account.

In so far as the above-mentioned submission of the applicants was intended to invite the Court to consider whether the orders committing them to prison had been made 'in excess of jurisdiction' even when those words did not appear on the face of the consent orders or judgments, the Court accepts that it is competent to consider whether the orders for detention were nevertheless made in excess of jurisdiction, while noting the submissions of the parties on this issue.

The Court recalls the above-cited § 44 of the Benham judgment in this context (i.e. that, as a result of section 108 of the Courts and Legal Services Act 1990, there was no reason for the High Court to decide whether the order had been made in excess of jurisdiction).

Admissible applications under Article 5

The Court considers that the complaints of 33 applicants involving the grounds set out below raise serious issues under Article 5 §§ 1 and 5 of the Convention which require determination on the merits. Directly below each of those grounds, the Court has listed the applications in which they arise. It follows that none of those applications can be dismissed as being manifestly ill-founded within the meaning of Article 35 § 3 of the Convention. No other ground for declaring the complaints under Article 5 §§ 1 and 5 in those applications inadmissible has been established.

The magistrates failed to conduct any or any proper means inquiry under regulation 41(2) of the 1989 Regulations

Kane (37706/97) Garnham (41593/98) Jones (46326/99)

Edwards (38260/97) Townsend (42039/98) Taylor (56231/00)

Hagyard (39378/98) Sheppard (45420/99) Christison (56429/00)

The magistrates failed to inquire as to the means/circumstances of the applicant for the period(s) when the debt(s) became due and/or failed to conduct separate inquiries under regulation 41(2) of the 1989 Regulations in respect of each liability order

Townsend (42039/98) Strickland (46140/99)
Mackman (47143/99) Wood (47441/99)

The magistrates failed to have proper regard to the alternatives to imprisonment in fines cases

Swaine (45844/99) Middleton (2483/03) Armstrong (55046/00)

Pitt (53111/99) Shelley (2484/03) Taylor (55071/00) Fletcher (2482/03)

Watson (54997/00)

The magistrates failed to ensure that a person under 21 years of age was given the opportunity to be legally represented

Ellis (42040/98) Taylor (56231/00)

The magistrates committed the applicant to prison in his or her absence without being satisfied that the applicant had received proper notice of the hearing

Lloyd (29798/96) Townsend (42039/98) Donald (56109/00) Kershaw-Field (36367/97)

Jones (46326/99) Reilly (56232/00) Barker (37551/97) Mason (47144/99)

Christison (56429/00) Kane (37706/97) Watts (53062/99) Wilson (56441/00)

Massey (38261/97) Watts (2490/03) Hagyard (39378/98) Jackson (55068/00)

The parties agreed on the face of the consent order that the magistrates failed to satisfy themselves that the conditions precedent to the issue of the committal warrants had been satisfied

Wood (47441/99)

The parties expressly agreed on the face of the consent order that the imprisonment of the applicant was unlawful

Swaine (45844/99)

The High Court held that the magistrates had lacked all power to issue the warrant of commitment

Parker (46416/99)

Inadmissible applications under Article 5

The Court notes that the applicant Waller (34327/96) has withdrawn his complaint under Article 5 of the Convention, accepting that the decisions of the magistrates in his case were not outside their jurisdiction.

The Court has determined the admissibility of the remaining applications with reference to the above-cited general principles that are set out at paragraphs 39-44 of its *Benham* judgment and at paragraph 62 of its *Perks* judgment. In each application considered below, the Court has had careful regard to the nature of the applicant's case, the terms of the consent order agreed between the parties, the domestic case-law referred to therein and the submissions and case-law provided by the parties.

Having carried out that examination, for the reasons expressed with greater particularity below, the Court is unable to conclude, with any degree of certainty, that the grounds for quashing the orders of the magistrates in any of the below applications established that the magistrates acted in excess of their jurisdiction within the meaning of domestic law. The Court, therefore, cannot find it established that the imprisonment orders were invalid and thus that the detention of the applicants which resulted from them was unlawful under national law.

The Court further notes that it has not been suggested in any of the below applications that the magistrates acted in bad faith. The Court does not find any other feature of those applications which could enable it to find that the detention of the applicant was arbitrary within the meaning of Article 5 of the Convention (see §§ 46 and 47 of the above-cited *Benham* judgment and

§§ 63 and 68-70 of the above-cited *Perks* judgment).

In those circumstances, it follows that the applicants' complaints under Article 5 § 1 are manifestly ill-founded within the meaning of Article 35 § 3 of the Convention and must be rejected pursuant to Article 35 § 4.

The Court observes that Article 5 § 5 of the Convention guarantees an enforceable right to compensation only to those who have been the victims of arrest or detention in contravention of the provisions of Article 5. In the light of its conclusion that the applicants' complaints under Article 5 § 1 are manifestly ill-founded in the below applications, the Court concludes that Article 5 § 5 is not applicable to their cases and that their complaints under that Article must therefore also be rejected as being manifestly ill-founded (see § 50 of the *Benham* judgment and § 74 of the *Perks* judgment).

Kenneth WOOD (30395/96)

The Court notes that the grounds for quashing the order in the present case were that the justices, in ordering the applicant's committal to prison, had been unreasonable in that they had failed to have regard to the change in the applicant's circumstances since their earlier order. The Court further notes that in its *Perks* judgment it found (at § 64), on the facts of that case, that the magistrates' failure to inquire into the change of the applicant's circumstances since their earlier order had been seen as a failure to take notice of a relevant piece of evidence and draw the ensuing conclusions, rather than as neglecting an express statutory condition precedent to their jurisdiction. No violation of Article 5 was therefore found. The Court does not have any material before it in the present case which could lead it to take a different view.

Indeed, the Court notes that the applicant does not specifically submit that the magistrates acted in excess of jurisdiction in his case. He instead relies upon his submissions to the effect that the test used in the *Benham* and *Perks* cases was wrong. For the reasons set out earlier in this decision, the Court rejects that submission.

G.M. (34341/96)

The Court notes that a finding of culpable neglect which could not be sustained on the available evidence has not been held sufficient to enable the Court to state with any degree of certainty that the resulting decision was outside the magistrates' jurisdiction within the meaning of domestic law (see §§ 45 and 46 of the above-cited *Benham* judgment). The Court considers ground (a) of the consent order in the present application to amount to a statement that the magistrates came to an unsustainable finding on the available evidence.

Even assuming, as the applicant submitted, that the reference to the *ex parte Stuart Martin* case could be interpreted as a finding that the magistrates applied the wrong standard of proof, the Court cannot be satisfied, to the requisite degree of certainty, that any such finding took the matter outside the magistrates' jurisdiction as opposed to being an error of law made within their jurisdiction.

The Court equally does not find it established that any jurisdictional issue arises in relation to ground (b) of the consent order. The Court recalls that in *Perks* (§ 67) it held that there was no sufficiently strong indication that the consideration of alternatives to imprisonment in community charge proceedings under the 1989 Regulations was regarded as a jurisdictional issue under domestic law. The applicant relied upon the same domestic case-law that was considered in *Perks* and upon the fact that he was imprisoned following his first hearing before the magistrates. The Court has taken account of those factors and does not find that there is any reason for it to come to a different conclusion from that which it reached in *Perks*.

The Court is also not satisfied, to the requisite degree of certainty, on the basis of the limited domestic case-law to which the applicant referred on the matter, that a failure to state reasons in the circumstances of this case (ground (c) of the consent order) or a failure to issue the committal warrant for the correct amount (ground (d)) amounted to errors which took the magistrates' decisions outside their jurisdiction within the meaning of domestic law, as opposed to being errors of law and/or an unreasonable exercise of discretion.

The Court notes finally that the magistrates in the present case agreed to bear the costs of the High Court application. Unlike the situation in which costs have been awarded against the magistrates during the course of a High Court judgment, the Court does not have any information before it which would enable it to determine the reasons behind the justices' agreement to bear the costs in this particular case. In those circumstances, the Court is not prepared to equate their agreement to pay the costs with a finding that their decision was in excess of jurisdiction.

Sanders (35445/97) and Condon (56233/00)

The Court is unable to conclude that the terms of the consent orders in either of the above applications establish that the magistrates acted in excess of their jurisdiction, as opposed to having incorrectly or unreasonably exercised the discretion that was vested in them.

The Court notes that the consent order in Sanders (35445/97) explicitly recognised that an order for deductions from income support (with which both these applications were concerned) was not one of the alternative enforcement steps that the justices were bound to consider under section 82(4A) of the Magistrates' Courts Act 1980.

Hughes (36267/97)

This applicant failed to provide the grounds upon which the decisions of the magistrates in his case were quashed, despite being requested to do so by the Court. In those circumstances, the Court finds his complaint under Article 5 of the Convention to be unsubstantiated.

Crilly (41590/98)

The Court recalls that the consent order recorded that the proceedings were not conducted in accordance with the principles of natural justice in that the clerk to the justices routinely retired with them when they considered the issue of a warrant of commitment. However, the Court has not been provided with any further information by the applicant about the circumstances of his case, in particular the occasions on which the clerk retired with the justices, the stage of the proceedings at which this occurred and why it was alleged that they were inappropriate. The applicant has also not made any submissions at all in relation to why he alleges that the order made by the justices was in excess of jurisdiction, whether by reference to domestic case-law or otherwise. The Court has, however, had regard to the domestic case cited in the consent order. It has not found anything in that case which could, without more, lead it to conclude, with a degree of certainty, that the matters complained of in this application amounted to a "gross and obvious procedural irregularity" or a finding that the magistrates had otherwise acted in excess of their jurisdiction. The Court further recalls that Lord Bridge expressly stated in the *McC* case that, even where there had been a breach of the rules of natural justice, that would not necessarily amount to the justices acting without or in excess of jurisdiction. His Lordship left that issue for determination on a case-by-case basis.

Hartley (42097/98)

The grounds for quashing the order of the justices in the current case were that they had failed sufficiently to take into account the change of circumstances of the applicant since the imposition of the term of imprisonment in their earlier order.

As such, the case raises similar issues to those that are considered in relation to Wood (30395/96) above, and the application is rejected for the same reasons.

Houghton (47985/99)

The Court recalls that the consent order in this application quashed the decision of the justices on the ground that to issue the warrant committing the applicant to prison in her absence and not to adjourn the proceedings in order to enable her to attend before them was unreasonable having regard to the evidence of her incapacity. This is therefore not a case in which it was agreed that the applicant had been committed to prison in her absence in circumstances in which the magistrates could not have been satisfied that she had received proper notice of the hearing.

The Court notes that the applicant has not provided any details about the evidence of her incapacity which is referred to in the order, nor has she elaborated further in any way about the circumstances surrounding her committal to prison in her absence, including what, if any, representations she had the opportunity of making to the justices in advance of the hearing of which she had notice (whether in relation to an adjournment or otherwise). The Court further notes that there is no reference to domestic case-law in relation to this ground on the face of the consent order, nor has the applicant referred to any domestic case-law in her submissions to the Court. In those circumstances, the Court does not have sufficient information which would enable it to conclude with a degree of certainty that the decision of the justices amounted to one which was taken in excess of jurisdiction within the meaning of domestic law, as opposed to one which was an unreasonable exercise of the discretion vested in them.

Slater (2460/03)

The Court recalls that the consent order in this case recorded that it was arguable that the magistrate had been unreasonable in ordering the applicant to be committed to prison without making any express reference to the possibility of deduction from income support.

The Court notes the terms of the order and the focus upon the lack of any "express reference" to the possibility of such a deduction. The Court further notes that this applicant was under 21 years of age at the time of his hearing before the magistrate.

The consent order does not specify in respect of which statutory provision, if any, the magistrate was arguably unreasonable; nor did the applicant make this clear. However, the Court recalls that section 1(5A) of the Criminal Justice Act 1982 requires a magistrates' court to state in open court its reasons for its opinions that no other method of dealing with a person under 21 years of age is appropriate when committing such a person to prison (see "Relevant domestic law" above). The Court further recalls that, in the *ex parte Cawley* case, it was specifically held that a failure to comply with the requirements of section 1(5A) did not render the order of committal to prison void, nor the detention under it unlawful, unless and until the warrant was quashed (see "Relevant domestic law" above). The Court cannot therefore conclude with any degree of certainty that the detention of the applicant, prior to the subsequent quashing of the committal order by the High Court (which occurred after the applicant had already been released on bail), was unlawful under domestic law.

Jelley (54969/00)

The Court recalls that the decision of the justices was quashed in the consent order as a result of their being unable to evidence from the face of the warrant or the records available at the court office what procedural steps they followed in committing the applicant to prison; and that, as a result of the time that had passed, it was difficult for them to recall events and therefore impossible for them to file affidavit evidence. The order stated that, in the light of the above-cited domestic case of *ex parte Cawley*, it was conceded by the justices that the High Court would be obliged to find in the applicant's favour. The Court further recalls that in the *ex parte Cawley* case it was specifically held that a warrant of commitment which was defective as a result of a failure to comply with the requirements under the relevant legislation to record the reasons why certain procedural steps were followed was not void and that therefore detention under it was not unlawful unless and until the warrant was quashed. The order does not state which procedural steps were not followed, nor does the applicant provide any details as to what these were. In those circumstances, the Court does not have any evidence whereby it could conclude that the justices took any step which rendered their decision in excess of jurisdiction.

Merry (54973/00)

The Court recalls that the decision of the justices to issue terms of imprisonment that would have hung over the applicant for nearly four years was quashed as being unreasonable. Having had regard to the domestic case-law referred to in the consent order and the case-law summarised under the heading "the length of the threat of imprisonment" in the above "Relevant domestic law" section, the Court cannot conclude with any degree of certainty that the error of the justices in the present case amounted to an act in excess of jurisdiction, as opposed to an error of law and/or an unreasonable exercise of the discretion which was vested in them.

<u>Article 6</u>

The applicants complained under Article 6 §§ 1 and 3(c) that they were not offered legal representation and were not represented at the hearing at which they were sentenced to a term of imprisonment.

Article 6 reads, insofar as relevant, as follows:

Article 6 - Right to a fair trial

> "1. In the determination of his civil rights and obligations or of any criminal charge against him, everyone is entitled to a fair and public hearing ...
>
> ...
>
> 3. Everyone charged with a criminal offence has the following minimum rights:
>
> ...

to defend himself in person or through legal assistance of his own choosing or, if he has not sufficient means to pay for legal assistance, to be given it free when the interests of justice so require".

(5) *The parties' submissions*

(a) **The Government**

The Government affirmed that the considerations relevant to the present complaints under Article 6 in relation to the availability of legal aid were examined by the Court in the *Benham* judgment at paragraphs 57-64 and in the *Perks* judgment at paragraphs 75-76.

The Government pointed out that legal aid was made available for such cases with effect from 1 June 1997. In the following applications the Government accepted that the relevant magistrates' court hearing had taken place before 1 June 1997 and that there was no feature to distinguish them from the findings in the *Benham* and *Perks* cases referred to:

Lloyd (29698/96), Wood (30395/96), Waller (34327/96), G.M.

(34341/96), Sanders (35445/97), Hughes (36267/97), Kershaw-Field (36367/97), Barker (37551/97), Kane (37706/97), Edwards (38260/97),

Massey (38261/97), Hagyard (39378/98), Crilly (41590/98), Garnham (41593/98), Townsend (42039/98), Hartley (42097/98), Swaine (45844/99), Wood (47441/99), Slater (2460/03), Fletcher (2482/03), Middleton (2483/03), Shelley (2484/03), Watts (2490/03), Pitt (53111/99), Jelley (54969/99), Merry (54973/99), Watson (54997/00), Armstrong (55046/00), Jackson (55068/00), Taylor (55071/00), Donald (56109/00) and Condon (56233/00).

The Government submitted, however, that there was no indication, whether in the order of the High Court or elsewhere, that any causal link was to be found between the lack of representation and the eventual detention of the applicant. The Government therefore questioned the utility of some of the foregoing applications where the legal principle had already been clearly established and, on the basis of previous Convention case-law, the only likely outcome, even if a violation were found, was an award of the costs and expenses incurred by the representative of the applicants.

The Government averred that in the *Perks* case the High Court had made a finding that Mr Perks was unlikely to have been detained had the magistrates known of his incapacity. The Government pointed out that no such finding or order had been made in any of the present cases in which the applicants alleged that there was a causal link between their lack of representation and their detention.

The Government stated that they disagreed with, and found hard to understand, the submission of the applicants that legal representation should have been available to them before the date on which their committal to prison was ordered.

Referring to the fact that legal aid was made available in this type of case with effect from 1 June 1997, the Government submitted that in relation to the following remaining applicants, whose hearings, they submitted, took place after that date, there had not been any violation of Article 6 § 3(c):

Ellis (42040/98), Sheppard (45420/99), Strickland (46140/99), Jones (46326/99), Parker (46416/99), Mackman (47143/99), Mason (47144/99), Houghton (47985/99), Watts (53062/99), Taylor (56231/00), Reilly (56232/00), Christison (56429/00) and Wilson (56441/00).

(b) **The applicants**

Raymond LLOYD (29798/96)

The applicant maintained that he should have been entitled to legal aid and that, had he been so entitled, the outcome of the proceedings would inevitably have been different. He referred to the fact that the judge in the High Court pointed out that the magistrates' court had been entitled to assistance from the Council's representative as to how they should have proceeded. The applicant referred to the judge having stated that common sense might have suggested an adjournment. The applicant therefore submitted that it was quite obvious that had the applicant been represented on that occasion his representative would have persuaded the court that the appropriate course of action was to adjourn until the applicant had the opportunity of obtaining benefit. The applicant further submitted that it was also quite obvious that had he been legally represented his representative would have persuaded the court that the order of 90 days' imprisonment suspended on payment of £20 a fortnight should not have been made.

In relation to the second hearing, the applicant pointed out that, as the judge was of the view that the court should not have been invited to proceed in circumstances where the warrant had been issued without there being proof of service, it was quite obvious that had he been represented his representative would have pointed out that defect to the court. In those circumstances, the effect of legal representation would have been that he would never have been imprisoned.

Robert WALLER (34327/96)

The applicant submitted that the unavailability of free legal representation in his case violated Article 6 §§ 1 and 3(c) of the Convention. He emphasised that he was wrongly sent to prison. He contended that, as was the case in *Perks*, he suffered from health problems, namely he had a long history of epilepsy.

He submitted that, had legal aid been available, his representative would inevitably have drawn the magistrates' attention to the defects that were made in their orders at his initial hearing; and his representative would also inevitably have drawn the attention of the magistrates to his ill-health and made representations as to why he should not have been committed to prison in his absence from his final hearing. In the circumstances, he submitted that it was unlikely that he would have been sent to prison had free legal representation been available to him.

The applicant further submitted that, had he been represented, his solicitors would inevitably have secured his release from prison on bail within a day or so of his committal rather than the fifty days that he actually spent in prison.

G.M. (34341/96)

The applicant maintained that he should have been entitled to legal representation and submitted that there was a clear causal link between its unavailability and his committal to prison. He argued that it was inconceivable that any competent solicitor would not have been aware of the many cases in the field that had by that time been decided by the High Court and brought them to the attention of the magistrates. The applicant further argued that, with such case-law before them, it was inconceivable that the magistrates would have made the errors set out in the consent order or committed him to prison, particularly as this was at the first hearing at which he had appeared before the court in this matter.

Anthony TOWNSEND (42039/98)

The applicant relied on the *Benham* case to submit that there had been a breach of Article 6 §§ 1 and 3(c) of the Convention in that legal aid was not available to him either at the hearing at which the justices found that he had culpably neglected to have paid his community charge and imposed a suspended term of imprisonment or at the subsequent hearing at which the magistrates activated that suspended sentence of imprisonment and sent him to prison in his absence. The applicant further submitted that, as in the case of *Perks*, the likelihood that he would have been committed to prison had he been represented would have been remote. The applicant referred to the fact that he had a history of psychiatric problems and had been an in-patient at a psychiatric hospital on a number of occasions.

The applicant further pointed out that at the time of his hearings before the magistrates he was in receipt of incapacity benefit, and that, on his reception to prison, he was transferred to the hospital wing of the prison. He submitted that it was inconceivable that, had he been represented, his representative would not have made submissions as to his health problems. He concluded that he should therefore be entitled to just satisfaction for the violation of Article 6 in his case for the same or similar reasons to those that applied to Mr Perks.

In his submissions in response to those of the Government, the applicant submitted for the first time that sending him to prison in his absence was contrary to Article 6 of the Convention. He relied on *Colozza v. Italy* (judgment of 12 February 1985, Series A no. 89) in this regard.

Mark WOOD (47441/99)

The applicant submitted that the lack of legal aid in relation to both the hearing of 28 February 1996 in which a suspended committal order was made, and the hearing of 10 March 1997 in which the committal warrant was issued, constituted a violation of Article 6 §§ 1 and 3(c). The applicant submitted that, given the nature of the proceedings and the penalty at stake, legal aid should have been available. He relied in this regard on the above- cited *Benham* case.

The applicant further submitted that there was a causal link between the lack of legal aid for representation and his committal to prison. He submitted that it was not in dispute that he was incapable of representing himself, he asked to be represented at court but was told that no representation was available and at the relevant time he was in receipt of income support. The applicant submitted that any competent representative would have been aware of the numerous reported and unreported cases that had been decided in the High Court by the time of his hearings, to which he referred. He argued that it was extremely unlikely that the justices would have committed him to prison as to do so would have necessitated the justices deliberately acting unlawfully in the light of the case-law that would have been shown to them. He therefore concluded that, as in the *Perks* case, it was 'beyond reasonable doubt' that, had he been represented, he would not have been committed to prison.

The remaining applicants

It was submitted on behalf of all of the remaining applicants that they were denied the opportunity of a fair and impartial hearing in accordance with the principles of Article 6 of the Convention.

All except Kane (37706/97), Mason (47144/99) and Taylor (55071/00) submitted that their cases were determined before the amendment to the law, which took effect on 1 June 1997, which provided for legal representation to be available under the legal aid scheme in cases of this nature. They submitted that they were not able to secure free legal representation at the hearings at which the magistrates inquired into their means, made a finding as to wilful refusal or culpable neglect and imposed a term of imprisonment (even if the issue of the warrant of imprisonment may have been postponed or suspended). The applicants submitted that it was at the initial hearing that the conditions precedent were established. They therefore submitted that if the Court were to find that committal in the applicants' absence was within the jurisdiction of the magistrates, then it was the decision at the initial hearing that would determine whether or not the decision to commit the applicant to prison was lawful. The applicants submitted that had the proceedings complied with the requirements of Article 6, they would not, in all likelihood, have been committed to prison. In the cases of Ellis (42040/98) and Houghton (47985/99) the applicants submitted that there was clear evidence that was available to the magistrates that they had good reason for failing to attend (the recorded delivery notice having been returned, and incapacity, respectively).

They argued that, had a properly briefed lawyer represented them at the hearing at which the warrant was issued, it was inconceivable that the magistrates would have issued the warrants in their absence.

In their response to the observations of the Government, it was submitted, for the first time, on behalf of applicants who had not been present at the second hearing at which they were committed to prison, that the fact of their absence, which denied them the opportunity to make representations to the court before the warrant of imprisonment was issued in their absence, constituted a violation of Article 6. Reference was made in this regard to the above-cited judgment in the case of *Colozza v. Italy*. The applicants' observations did not specify by name or application number the applicants on whose behalf this submission was made.

The Court's assessment

(c) The submissions under Article 6 concerning applicants whose committal orders were issued in their absence

As noted above, with the exception of Townsend (42039/98), it was not specified on behalf of which applicants the submission was made that the fact of their absence from the hearing at which the committal warrant was issued constituted a violation of Article 6. The Court is aware that the committal orders in certain applications were quashed on the grounds of the applicant's absence from the final hearing (see the table relating to the circumstances of the cases below). The Court notes that the tabular submissions on behalf of those applicants represented by Dicksons HMB Solicitors (see above) referred to additional applicants as having been committed in their absence, even where there was not any mention of that factor in the High Court consent orders. For the avoidance of doubt, the reasoning of the Court which follows below applies to all applicants on whose behalf it was intended to submit that the fact of their absence violated Article 6.

The Court notes that the submission that an applicant's absence from the hearing at which the committal warrant was issued constituted a violation of Article 6 was made for the first time in the observations of the applicants filed in response to those of the Government about the admissibility and merits of these applications. Prior to that time, none of the applicants had at any stage indicated that they were complaining under Article 6 of the Convention about the fact that their committal took place in their absence.

Their complaints under Article 6 were as set out under the heading "Complaints" above. The Court further notes that the applicants have at all times been legally represented in their proceedings before this Court and that their applications to the Court (which require a statement of the alleged violations of the Convention and the relevant arguments in respect thereof) were prepared and submitted to the Court by lawyers.

The Court recalls the requirement under Article 35 § 1 of the Convention for the matter to be brought before it within a period of six months from the date on which the final domestic decision was taken in the process of the exhaustion of domestic remedies.

As such, the applicants' complaint under Article 6 about the fact that their committal orders were issued in their absence is inadmissible for having failed to comply with the six months requirement under Article 35 § 1 of the Convention.

(d) **Admissible applications under Article 6 §§ 1 and 3(c)**

The Court considers that the applicants' complaints under Article 6 §§ 1 and 3(c), in the specific circumstances described in the headings below, raise serious issues under that Article which require determination on the merits. Directly below each of those headings, the Court has listed the applications in which they arise. It follows that none of those applications can be dismissed as being manifestly ill-founded within the meaning of Article 35 § 3 of the Convention. No other ground for declaring the complaints under Article 6 §§ 1 and 3(c) in those applications inadmissible has been established.

Where the proceedings as a whole took place before 1 June 1997

Lloyd (29798/96) Hagyard (39378/98) Shelley (2484/03) Wood (30395/96) Crilly (41590/98) Watts (2490/03) Waller (34327/96) Garnham (41593/98) Jelley (54969/00) G.M. (34341/96) Townsend (42039/98) Merry (54973/00) Sanders (35445/97) Hartley (42097/98) Watson (54997/00) Hughes (36267/97) Swaine (45844/99) Armstrong (55046/00) Kershaw-Field (36367/97) Wood (47441/99) Jackson (55068/00) Barker (37551/97) Pitt (53111/99) Taylor (55071/00) Kane (37706/97) Slater (2460/03) Donald (56109/00) Edwards (38260/97) Fletcher (2482/03) Condon (56233/00) Massey (38261/97) Middleton (2483/03)

Where a term of imprisonment was fixed, albeit postponed on terms, at a hearing which took place before 1 June 1997

Massey (38261/97) Strickland (46140/99) Watts (53062/99) Sheppard (45420/99) Mackman (47143/99) Reilly (56232/00)

Where a term of imprisonment was imposed on a person under 21 years of age who was not legally represented

Ellis (42040/98) Taylor (56231/00)

(e) *Inadmissible applications under Article 6 §§ 1 and 3(c)*

(6) The Court recalls that, as from 1 June 1997, free legal representation was made available by the Government in respect of the types of proceedings under consideration in this decision (see "Relevant domestic law" above). In the applications listed below, both hearings in respect of the adult applicants' committal to prison took place after 1 June 1997. As such, the applicants were entitled to apply for free legal representation. There is no indication in their applications that they did so. There is equally no suggestion that they were refused legal representation having requested it, nor that they were prevented from informing themselves as to the representation options available to them. In those circumstances, the Court finds their complaint under Article 6 that they were neither offered legal representation nor represented to be manifestly ill-founded within the meaning of Article 35 § 3 of the Convention.

The Court therefore rejects the following applications under Article 6, pursuant to Article 35 § 4 of the Convention:

Jones (46326/99) Mason (47144/99) Christison (56429/00) Parker (46416/99)

Houghton (47985/99) Wilson (56441/00)

Recapitulation

For these reasons, the Court unanimously

Declares the following application inadmissible:

Houghton (47985/99)

Declares admissible, without prejudging the merits, the applicant's complaints under Article 5 §§ 1 and 5 of the Convention, in the following applications

Lloyd (29798/96) Swaine (45844/99) Shelley (2484/03)

Kershaw-Field (36367/97) Strickland (46140/99) Watts (2490/03)

Barker (37551/97) Jones (46326/99) Watson (54997/00) Kane (37706/97)

Parker (46416/99) Armstrong (55046/00) Edwards (38260/97)

Mackman (47143/99) Jackson (55068/00) Massey (38261/97)

Mason (47144/99) Taylor (55071/00) Hagyard (39378/98)

Wood (47441/99) Donald (56109/00) Garnham (41593/98) Watts (53062/99)

Taylor (56231/00) Townsend (42039/98) Pitt (53111/99) Reilly (56232/00)

Ellis (42040/98) Fletcher (2482/03) Christison (56429/00)

Sheppard (45420/99) Middleton (2483/03) Wilson (56441/00)

Declares inadmissible the applicant's complaints under Article 5 §§ 1 and 5 of the Convention in the following applications:

Wood (30395/96) Hughes (36267/97) Jelley (54969/00) Waller (34327/96)

Crilly (41590/98) Merry (54973/00) G.M. (34341/96) Hartley (42097/98)

Condon (56233/00) Sanders (35445/97) Slater (2460/03)

Declares admissible, without prejudging the merits, the applicant's complaints under Article 6 §§ 1 and 3(c) of the Convention, in the following applications:

Lloyd (29798/96) Garnham (41593/98) Middleton (2483/03)Wood (30395/96)

Townsend (42039/98) Shelley (2484/03) Waller (34327/96) Ellis (42040/98)

Watts (2490/03) G.M. (34341/96) Hartley (42097/98) Jelley (54969/00)

Sanders (35445/97)Sheppard (45420/99) Merry (54973/00)Hughes (36267/97)

Swaine (45844/99) Watson (54997/00) Kershaw-Field(36367/97)Strickland (46140/99)

Armstrong(55046/00) Barker (37551/97) Mackman (47143/99) Jackson (55068/00)

Kane (37706/97) Wood (47441/99) Taylor (55071/00) Edwards (38260/97)

Watts (53062/99) Donald (56109/00) Massey (38261/97)Pitt (53111/99)

Taylor (56231/00) Hagyard (39378/98) Slater (2460/03) Reilly (56232/00)

Crilly (41590/98) Fletcher (2482/03) Condon (56233/00)

Declares inadmissible the applicant's complaints under Article 6 §§ 1 and 3(c) of the Convention in the following applications:

Jones (46326/99)

Mason (47144/99)

Wilson (56441/00) Parker

(46416/99)

Christison (56429/00)

Declares inadmissible the complaint under Article 6 relating to the absence of the applicant from the hearing at which the committal warrant was issued, in respect of each applicant on whose behalf it was intended to raise that complaint.

Michael O'BOYLE
Registrar

Matti PELLONPÄÄ
President

Raymond LLOYD 29798/96 Days in prison Thirty- six before 1st June

1997 Grounds why order quashed:

Notes of the judgment of Mr Justice Turner of 2 November 1995

"On 21 July 1994 ... the applicant went before the Justices and ... stated he did not refuse to pay but could not and offered £5 to £10 per week depending on how much benefit he received. The magistrates were entitled to assistance from the representative of North Hertfordshire District Council as to how they should have proceeded. It is plain although the Justices were entitled to find culpable neglect (there is no issue on that) common sense might have suggested an adjournment until the applicant applied for and received benefit. There is nothing to suggest that the North Hertfordshire District Council representative sought to persuade the Justices to adjourn or sought to deter the magistrates from the order they made, namely committal for 90 days suspended on payment of £20 per fortnight. That order should not have been made.

On 22 December 1994 ... a warrant was issued ... the Justices should not have been invited to proceed without there being evidence that the recall notice had been validly served [on the applicant]."

Kenneth WOOD 30395/96 Days in prison Seven before 1st June1997

Grounds why order quashed:

"The Justices, in ordering the applicant's committal to prison on 1st March 1995 were UNREASONABLE in that they failed to have regard to the change in the Applicant's circumstances since the earlier order of 18th August 1994."

Robert WALLER 34327/96 Days in prison Fifty before 1st June 1997

Grounds why order quashed:

"(a) The Justices erred in law on 18th March 1992 in fixing an excessive term of imprisonment, see *R. v. Highbury Corner Magistrates' Court ex parte Uchendu* [1994] RA 51.

(b) The Justices erred in law on 14th July 1994 in fixing the maximum sentence available to them, see *R. v. Mid-Hertfordshire Justices ex parte Leslie Cox*, unreported, 19th October 1995."

G.M. 34341/96 Days in prison Ten before 1June 1997

Grounds why order quashed:

"(a) The Justices erred in finding the Applicant to have wilfully refused and culpably neglected to have paid his community charge in the light of the letter from the Applicant's solicitor read to them, see *R v. South Tyneside Justices ex parte Stuart Martin*, unreported, 20 September 1995,
In committing the applicant to a term of imprisonment at the first hearing of this matter the Justices failed to have proper regard to the purpose of imprisonment in such cases, see *R v. Wolverhampton Magistrates Court ex parte Mould* [1992] RA 309
The Justices erred in failing to give reasons for their decision, and
The Justices erred in issuing the committal warrant for the wrong amount, see *R v. Erewash Borough Council and Ilkeston Justices ex parte Smedberg and Smedberg* [1994] RVR 60."

The Justices agreed to pay the costs of the applicant's application for judicial review

SANDERS 35445/97 Days in prison Three before 1st June 1997

Grounds why order quashed:

"In the light of the applicant's evidence that she was in receipt of income support and although an order for deduction from income support ("a deduction order") is not one of the alternative enforcement steps the justices are bound by section 82(4A) Magistrates' Courts Act 1980 to consider it is accepted that the justices, in seeking to enforce the amounts outstanding, could have exercised their discretion to make a deduction order."

Clive HUGHES 36267/97 Days in prison Five before 1st June 1997

Grounds why order quashed:

(*The applicant's solicitors were requested by the Court by letter of 13 April 2000 to provide the grounds upon which the magistrates' orders were quashed by 15 May 2000. No grounds have ever been provided.*)

Marguerita KERSHAW- FIELD 36367/97 Days in prison Two before 1st June 1997

Grounds why order quashed:

"(i) The Justices were unlawful in committing the applicant to an immediate term of imprisonment in that they failed to have proper regard to the purpose of imprisonment in such cases see *R v. Alfreton Justices ex parte Gratton* CO/484/93, transcript at page 4 per Mr Justice Macpherson of Cluny, ' ... we all know now as a result of a number of decisions that community charge liability should only be visited with prison ... if there is no other way in which the money can be extracted. Prison is not to be used as a big stick or primarily as punishment, but as a means of extracting the liability.'"

The Justices were unlawful in committing the Applicant to an immediate term of imprisonment in her absence in that they could not have been satisfied that the applicant had received proper notice of the hearing see Mr Justice Jowitt in *R v. Hyndburn Justices ex parte Woolaghan* [unreported 2nd December 1995] "The difficulty, though, for the Magistrates is, that when there is no appearance before them, they really have no way of telling whether this may be one of those, no doubt no[t] over-frequent cases in which a letter has miscarried for one reason or another, perhaps because it has not been delivered or because the charge payer is absent for a continuing period from home, or because, in premises with a number of separate occupiers, a letter has got into the wrong hands. It seems, therefore, to follow that where there has been service by ordinary post, careful consideration would have to be given to the particular circumstances of the charge payer, before, if ever, concluding that the notice must have come into his hands ... there being no proof of service ... the applicant is entitled to succeed and the Order of Certiorari must go to quash the committal warrant" and *R v. Northampton Magistrates Court ex parte New[e]ll* [1992] CA RA 83.

In view of the applicant's circumstances, the time that has elapsed since the applicant was imprisoned and the period of time spent in prison, all parties agree that this matter be not remitted to the Magistrates, in accordance with the principles outlined by Lord Justice Watkins in *R v. Crewe and Nantwich Magistrates ex parte Burton* CO/3095/92 and *R v. Felixstowe Justices ex parte Haddow* [1992] RA 245."

John BARKER 37551/97 Days in prison Twenty Eight before 1st June 1997

Grounds why order quashed:

"(i) The Justices were unreasonable in committing the applicant to the maximum period of imprisonment on the 5th February 1992, see *R v. Highbury Corner Magistrates' Court ex parte Uchendu* (CO/2351/93) and further relying on the original term imposed and failing to revise the term of imprisonment imposed when the warrant was issued on the 13th May 1992, see Lord Donaldson MR in *R*
v. Northampton Justices ex parte New[e]ll [1992] RA 283 at 292: "I agree that section 12 of the Interpretation Act 1978 would empower the magistrates to repeat the whole reg 41(3) stage by considering afresh whether to issue a warrant of commitment against the debtor or to fix a new term of imprisonment and to postpone the warrant for the same or a different time and on the same or different conditions."

The Justices were unreasonable in committing the applicant to a period of imprisonment of 90 days in respect of Community Charge arrears on the 5th February 1992, placing the applicant in an inferior position to a person convicted of a criminal offence and being subject to the limitations of Schedule 4 of the Magistrates' Courts Act 1980 see *R v. Southampton Justices ex parte*

Davies [1981] 1 WLR 374 and further relying on the original term imposed and failing to revise the term of imprisonment imposed when the warrant was issued on the 13th May 1992.
the Justices were unlawful in committing the applicant to an immediate term of imprisonment in his absence in that they could not have been satisfied that the applicant had received proper notice of the hearing see Mr. Justice Jowitt in *R v. Hyndburn Justices ex parte Woolag[h]an* [unreported 2nd December 1995]: "The difficulty, though, for the Magistrates is, that when there is no appearance before them, they really have no way of telling whether this may be one of those, no doubt not over frequent cases in which a letter has miscarried for one reason or another, perhaps because it has not been delivered or because the charge payer is absent for a continuing period from home, or because, in premises with a number of separate occupiers, a letter has got into the wrong hands. It seems therefore, to follow that where there has been service by ordinary post, careful consideration would have to be given to the particular circumstances of the charge payer, before, if ever, concluding that the notice must have come into his hands ... there being no proof of service ... the applicant is entitled to succeed and the Order of Certiorari must go to quash the committal warrant" and *R v. Northampton Magistrates Court Ex parte New[e]ll* [1992] CA RA 83.
in view of the applicant's circumstances, the time that has elapsed since the applicant was imprisoned and the period of time spent in prison, all parties agree that this matter be not remitted to the Magistrates."

Angela KANE 37706/97 Days in prison Four before 1st June 1997

Grounds why order quashed:

"(i) the Justices were unlawful committing the applicant to a period of imprisonment in respect of her Community Charge liability without having conducted a proper enquiry into her means. Regulation 41(2) of the Community Charge (Administration and Enforcement) Regulations requires that the Magistrate inquire, in the defaulter's presence, as to whether the failure to pay which led to the Liability Order being made was due to her wilful refusal or culpable neglect, failure to make adequate inquiry will render any decision to commit to prison, suspended or otherwise, unlawful see Mr Justice Laws in *R v. Stafford Justices ex parte Johnson* (CO/1467/94) "any reasonable bench of Justices must have realised, the means inquiry required by Regulation 41(2) is of great importance because without it the Justices plainly cannot properly arrive at a conclusion as to whether the failure to pay had been due to the debtor's wilful refusal or culpable neglect. A means inquiry, thus, is at the centre of the enforcement procedure which is laid down by these Regulations. The[se] Justices did not, in truth, embark upon a proper means inquiry at all. It follows that their order committing the applicant to prison is entirely vitiated." The applicant avers that the Justices were unable to make any finding of wilful refusal or culpable neglect any enquiry into the applicant's means must be to the higher "beyond reasonable doubt" standard of proof (see Mr Justice Sedley in *R v. South Tyneside Magistrates ex parte Stuart Martin* (CO/1755/94), there was no cogent evidence of her wilful refusal or culpable neglect as of the time that the Community Charge liability became due in order to enable the Justices to issue a warrant of commitment, postponed or otherwise.
the Justices were unreasonable in committing the applicant to a period of imprisonment of 28 days in respect of Community Charge arrears of £228.63 placing the applicant in an inferior position to a person convicted of a criminal offence and being subject to the limitations of Schedule 4 of the Magistrates' Courts Act 1980 see *R v. Southampton Justices ex parte Davies* [1981] 1 WLR 374.
the Justices were unlawful in that they failed to review the basis upon which the term of imprisonment was passed upon having heard evidence of the applicant's change of circumstances see *R v. Mid Herts Justices ex parte Cox* CO/3584/94.

the Justices were unlawful in committing the applicant to an immediate term of imprisonment in her absence in that they could not have been satisfied that the applicant had received proper notice of the hearing see Mr. Justice Jowitt in *R v. Hyndburn Justices ex parte Woolag[h]an* [unreported 2nd December 1995] "The difficulty, though, for the Magistrates is, that when there is no appearance before them, they really have no way of telling whether this may be one of those, no doubt not over frequent cases in which a letter has miscarried for one reason or another, perhaps because it has not been delivered or because the charge payer is absent for a continuing period from home, or because, in premises with a number of separate occupiers, a letter has got into the wrong hands. It seems therefore, to follow that where there has been service by ordinary post, careful consideration would have to be given to the particular circumstances of the charge payer, before, if ever, concluding that the notice must have come into his hands ... there being no proof of service ... the applicant is entitled to succeed and the Order of Certiorari must go to quash the committal warrant" and *R v. Northampton Magistrates Court Ex parte New[e]ll* [1992] CA RA 83.
(v) in view of the applicant's circumstances, the time that has elapsed since the applicant was imprisoned and the period of time spent in prison, all parties agree that this matter be not remitted to the Magistrates."

Caroline EDWARDS 38260/97 Days in prison Two before 1st June 1997

Grounds why order quashed:
"(i) the Justices were unlawful in making a finding that the applicant had culpably neglected to pay her Community Charge without conducting an enquiry into [her] conduct as of the time that the liability became due. Regulation 41(2) of the Community Charge (Administration and Enforcement) Regulations requires that the Magistrate inquire, in the defaulter's presence, as to whether the failure to pay which led to the Liability Order being made was due to her wilful refusal or culpable neglect, failure to make adequate inquiry will render any decision to commit to prison, suspended or otherwise, unlawful see Mr Justice Laws in *R v. Stafford Justices ex parte Johnson* (CO/1467/94) "any reasonable bench of Justices must have realised, the means inquiry required by Regulation 41(2) is of great importance because without it the Justices plainly cannot properly arrive at a conclusion as to whether the failure to pay had been due to the debtor's wilful refusal or culpable neglect. A means inquiry, thus, is at the centre of the enforcement procedure which is laid down by these Regulations. The[se] Justices did not, in truth, embark upon a proper means inquiry at all. It follows that their order committing the applicant to prison is entirely vitiated." Having regard to the consequences of any finding of wilful refusal or culpable neglect any enquiry into the applicant's means must be to the higher "beyond reasonable doubt" standard of proof (see Mr Justice Sedley in *R v. South Tyneside Magistrates ex parte Stuart Martin* (CO/1755/94), there must therefore be cogent evidence of the applicant's wilful refusal or culpable neglect as of the time that the Community Charge liability became due before the Justices can issue a warrant of commitment, postponed or otherwise.
(ii) the Justices were unlawful in issuing a warrant of commitment for 14 days, failing to take into account the payments made by the applicant as a result of the failure of the prosecuting Charging Authority to bring details of the applicant's payments to the notice of the Justices.

(iii) in view of the applicant's circumstances, the time that has elapsed since the applicant was imprisoned and the period of time spent in prison, all parties agree that this matter be not remitted to the Magistrates, in accordance with the principles outlined by Lord Justice Watkins in *R v. Crewe and Nantwich Magistrates ex parte Burton* CO/3095/92 and *R v. Felixstow Justices ex parte Haddow* [1992] RA 245."

Robert MASSEY 38261/97 Days in prison Three and Two both [1] <u>before</u> 1st June 1997

Grounds why order quashed:

The applicant complains in respect of two separate sets of proceedings. In respect of the first set of proceedings:

"(i) the justices acted unlawfully in issuing the commitment warrant as the notice given to the applicant of the hearing on 16th September 1994 was sent by ordinary post and the justices were therefore wrong in concluding, in the absence of an acknowledgment, that the notice must have come into the applicant's hands (see *R v. Hyndburn Justices ex parte Woolaghan* [unreported 2nd December 1994].

(ii) In view of the time that has elapsed since the applicant was sentenced to imprisonment and the period spent in prison, all parties agree that the justices decision be quashed and that a term of imprisonment equal to that already served be substituted for the balance of the original term in accordance with the principles outlined by Lord Justice Watkins in *R v. Crewe and Nantwich Magistrates ex parte Burton* CO/3095/92 and *R v. Felixstowe Justices ex parte Haddow* [1992] RA 245" **In respect of the second set of proceedings:**

"The Justices having found culpable neglect, the decision to commit to prison for 28 days suspended on payment of £15.00 per month is bad on the face of it as the period of payment is disproportionately heavy: *R v. Newcastle upon Tyne Justices ex parte Devine* [1998] RA 97."

[1] The word "both" signifies that the hearing at which the term of imprisonment was fixed, and then postponed on terms, occurred before 1 June 1997, but the hearing at which the warrant of committal was issued and the applicant was sent to prison occurred after 1 June 1997.

HAGYARD 39378/98 Days in prison Two before 1st June 1997

Grounds why order quashed:

"(i) the Justices were unlawful committing the applicant to a period of imprisonment in respect of her Community Charge liability without having conducted a proper enquiry into her means. Regulation 41(2) of the Community Charge (Administration and Enforcement) Regulations requires that the Magistrate inquire, in the defaulter's presence, as to whether the failure to pay which led to the Liability Order being made was due to her wilful refusal or culpable neglect, failure to make adequate inquiry will render any decision to commit to prison, suspended or otherwise, unlawful see Mr Justice Laws in *R v. Stafford Justices ex parte Johnson* (CO/1467/94) "any reasonable bench of Justices must have realised, the means inquiry required by Regulation 41(2) is of great importance because without it the Justices plainly cannot properly arrive at a conclusion as to whether the failure to pay had been due to the debtor's wilful refusal or culpable neglect. A means inquiry, thus, is at the centre of the enforcement procedure which is laid down by these Regulations. The[se] Justices did not, in truth, embark upon a proper means inquiry at all. It follows that their order committing the applicant to prison is entirely vitiated." The applicant avers that the Justices were unable to make any finding of wilful refusal or culpable neglect any enquiry into the applicant's means must be to the higher "beyond reasonable doubt" standard of proof (see Mr Justice Sedley in *R v. South Tyneside Magistrates ex parte Stuart Martin* (CO/1755/94), there was no cogent evidence of her wilful refusal or culpable neglect as of the time that the Community Charge liability became due in order to enable the Justices to issue a warrant of commitment, postponed or otherwise.

the Justices were unreasonable in committing the applicant to a period of imprisonment of 14 days in respect of Community Charge arrears of £213.45 placing the applicant in an inferior position to a person convicted of a criminal offence and being subject to the limitations of Schedule 4 of the Magistrates Court Act 1980.

the Justices were unlawful in committing the applicant to an immediate term of imprisonment in her absence in that they could not have been satisfied that the applicant had received proper notice of the hearing see Mr. Justice Jowitt in *R v. Hyndburn Justices ex parte Woolag[h]an* [unreported 2nd December 1995] "The difficulty, though, for the Magistrates is, that when there is no appearance before them, they really have no way of telling whether this may be one of those, no doubt not over frequent cases in which a letter has miscarried for one reason or another, perhaps because it has not been delivered or because the charge payer is absent for a continuing period from home, or because, in premises with a number of separate occupiers, a letter has got into the wrong hands. It seems therefore, to follow that where there has been service by ordinary post, careful consideration would have to be given to the particular circumstances of the charge payer, before, if ever, concluding that the notice must have come into his hands ... there being no proof of service ... the applicant is entitled to succeed and the Order of Certiorari must go to quash the committal warrant" and *R v. Northampton Magistrates Court Ex parte New[e]ll* [1992] CA RA 83.

HAGYARD 39378/98 (continued) Days in prison Two before 1st June 1997

Grounds why order quashed:

(iv) in view of the applicant's circumstances, and the circumstances of the applicant's six children under 11, the time that has elapsed since the applicant was imprisoned and the period of time spent in prison, all parties agree that this matter be not remitted to the Magistrates."

David CRILLY 41590/98 Days in prison Fifteen before 1st June 1997

Grounds why order quashed:

"(i) the proceedings before the South Ribble Justices were not conducted in accordance with the principles of natural justice in that the Clerk to the Justices routinely retired with the Justices when considering the issue of a warrant of commitment in connection with the applicant's fines default see *Practice Direction (Justices Clerks)* [1953] 1 WLR 1416;

(ii) in view of the applicant's circumstances, the time that has elapsed since the applicant was imprisoned and the time spent in prison, all parties agree that this matter be not remitted to the Magistrates."

Joan GARNHAM 41593/98 Days in prison Two before 1st June 1997

Grounds why order quashed:
"(i) the Justices were wrong in committing the applicant to a period of imprisonment in respect of her Community Charge liability without having conducted a proper enquiry into her means as of the time the respective liabilities became due (see *R v. Leeds ex parte Kennett* [1996] RVR 53, *R v. Durham City Justices ex parte Fleming* CO/2023/98). Regulation 41(2) of the Community Charge (Administration and Enforcement) Regulations requires that the Magistrate make a finding, in the defaulter's presence, as to whether the failure to pay which led to the Liability Order being made was due to her wilful refusal or culpable neglect, failure to make adequate inquiry will render any decision to commit to prison, suspended or otherwise, unlawful see Mr Justice Laws in *R v. Stafford Justices ex parte Johnson* (CO/1467/94) "any reasonable bench of Justices must have realised, the means inquiry required by Regulation 41(2) is of great importance because without it the Justices plainly cannot properly arrive at a conclusion as to whether the failure to pay had been due to the debtor's wilful refusal or culpable neglect. A means inquiry, thus, is at the centre of the enforcement procedure which is laid down by these Regulations. The[se] Justices did not, in truth, embark upon a proper means inquiry at all. It follows that their order committing the applicant to prison is entirely vitiated." The applicant avers that the Justices were unable to make any finding of wilful refusal or culpable neglect any enquiry into the applicant's means must be to the higher "beyond reasonable doubt" standard of proof (see Mr Justice Sedley in *R v. South Tyneside Magistrates ex parte Stuart Martin* (CO/1755/94), there was no cogent evidence of her wilful refusal or culpable neglect as of the time that the Community Charge liability became due in order to enable the Justices to issue a warrant of commitment, postponed or otherwise.

(ii) in view of the applicant's circumstances, the time that has elapsed since the applicant was imprisoned and the period of time spent in prison, all parties agree that this matter be not remitted to the Magistrates."

Anthony TOWNSEND 42039/98 Days in prison Seven before 1st June 1997

Grounds why order quashed:
"(i) The Justices failed to conduct a proper or any enquiry into the Applicant's means as required by Regulation 41(2) Community Charge (Administration and Enforcement) Regulations 1989. The means enquiry required by Regulation 41(2) of the 1989 Regulations is "at the centre of the enforcement procedure which is laid down by these Regulations" per Mr Justice Laws in *R v. Stafford Justices ex parte Shaun Thomas Johnson,* 16th March 1995. A failure to conduct such a means enquiry will render any subsequent committal to prison unlawful.
The Justices failed to conduct proper or any enquiries into the Applicant's circumstances leading to the grant of the Liability Orders. A failure to conduct an enquiry into a debtor's circumstances leading to each liability made against them will render any decision to find

culpable neglect or wilful refusal flawed as per *R v. Leeds Justices ex parte Kennett* [1996] RVR 53.
The Justices could not have been satisfied to the requisite standard of proof that the Applicant had culpably neglected to have paid the sums due. See *R v. South Tyneside Justices ex parte Martin*. Unreported 31st July 1995.
The Justices' decision on the 18th April 1996 was unlawful in that they could not have been satisfied that the Applicant had received a notice of the hearing of Summons to attend before the Justices on that date. Before committing a debtor to Prison the Rules of Natural Justice require that he be given the opportunity to make representations to the Court. See *R v. Northampton Magistrates Court ex parte Newell* [1992] RA 283. Further, the Justices considering an application to commit a debtor to prison are required to be satisfied that the debtor received a notice or Summons to attend. See *R v. Hyndburn Justices ex parte Woolaghan,* unreported to 2.12.1994."

Paul ELLIS 42040/98 Days in prison Eight After 1st June 1997
Grounds why order quashed:
The applicant was under 21 years of age at the time of his hearings before the magistrates.
"(i) the Justices are unable to refute the applicant's ground for a Judicial Review of the decision that the Justices had acted unlawfully failed to consider and communicate in open court and upon the warrant of commitment the reasons why all other methods of enforcement were considered to be unreasonable or impracticable.
(ii) the Justices are unable to refute the applicant's grounds for a Judicial Review of the decision that the Justices had unlawfully failed to ensure that he was given the opportunity to be legally represented at the hearings when they considered matters concerning his liberty".

Maxine HARTLEY 42097/98 Days in prison Three Before 1st June 1997
Grounds why order quashed:
"(i) the decision of the Justices to issue the warrant of commitment failed to sufficiently take into account the applicant's change of circumstances since the imposition of the term of imprisonment.
(ii) in view of the circumstances of the applicant, and the period of detention served, the matter be not remitted back to the Magistrates."

Sharon SHEPPARD 45420/99 Days in prison Two both Before 1st June 1997
Grounds why order quashed:
"(i) the decision of the Justices to sentence the applicant to a period of imprisonment in respect of her Community Charge liability without having conducted a proper enquiry into her means as of the time the respective liabilities became due was unlawful (see *R v. Leeds ex parte Kennett* [1996] RVR 53, *R v. Durham City Justices ex parte Fleming* CO/2023/96). Regulation 41(2) of the Community Charge (Administration and Enforcement) Regulations requires that the Magistrate make a finding, in the defaulter's presence, as to whether the failure to pay which led to the Liability Order being made was due to her wilful refusal or culpable neglect, failure to make adequate inquiry will render any decision to commit to prison, suspended or otherwise, unlawful see Mr Justice Laws in *R v. Stafford Justices ex parte Johnson* (CO/1467/94) "any reasonable

bench of Justices must have realised, the means inquiry required by Regulation 41(2) is of great importance because without it the Justices plainly cannot properly arrive at a conclusion as to whether the failure to pay had been due to the debtor's wilful refusal or culpable neglect. A means inquiry, thus, is at the centre of the enforcement procedure which is laid down by these Regulations. The[se] Justices did not, in truth, embark upon a proper means inquiry at all. It follows that their order committing the applicant to prison is entirely vitiated." The applicant avers that the Justices were unable to make any finding of wilful refusal or culpable neglect any enquiry into the applicant's means must be to the higher "beyond reasonable doubt" standard of proof (see Mr Justice Sedley in *R v. South Tyneside Magistrates ex parte Stuart Martin* (CO/1755/94), there was no cogent evidence of her wilful refusal or culpable neglect as of the time that the Community Charge liability became due in order to enable the Justices to issue a warrant of commitment, postponed or otherwise.
(ii) in view of the applicant's circumstances, the time that has elapsed since the applicant was imprisoned and the period of time spent in prison, all parties agree that this matter be not remitted to the Magistrates."

Mitchell SWAINE 45844/99 Days in prison Three before 1st June 1997
Grounds why order quashed:

The applicant was under 21 years of age at the time of his hearings before the magistrates.
"(i) the Justices were unlawful in committing the applicant to an immediate term of imprisonment without having regard to the provisions of section 88 of the Magistrates' Courts Act, see Simon Brown LJ in *Re: Cawley and Others* (CO/1832/95), 28th November 1995 transcript at page 28 "...it must be possible to see from the [face] of the warrant (and register) why it is that, very exceptionally one hopes, the Justices have felt no alternative but to commit this young person to custody" in particular as to why the alternatives of a Fines Supervision Order or deductions from Income Support would have been inappropriate or unsuccessful.
(ii) in view of the circumstances of the applicant, the unlawfulness of his imprisonment and the period of detention served the matter be not remitted back to the Magistrates."

Sandra STRICKLAND 46140/99 Days in prison Three both before 1st June 1997
Grounds why order quashed:

"(i) The decisions of the Justices on 1st November 1994, 30th July 1996 and 25th November 1997 when they found that the failure of the applicant to pay the debts due in respect of non-payment of non-domestic rates for four properties on the Isle of Wight ... were wrong in law in that the Justices failed to enquire as to the means of the applicant for the relevant periods when the debts became due contrary to *Regulation 16(2) of the Non-Domestic Rating [Collection etc] Regulations 1989* and the principles laid down in *R v. Leeds Justices ex parte Kennett* [1996] RVR 53.
(ii) Consequently the decisions of the justices to issue warrants committing the applicant to prison for non-payment of the said debts were unlawful."

Angela JONES 46326/99 Days in prison Three After 1st June 1997
Grounds why order quashed:
"(i) the decision of the Justices to commit the applicant to a period of imprisonment in respect of her Council Tax liability without having conducted a proper enquiry into her means was unlawful (Ground C) see Mr Justice Laws in *R v. Stafford Justices ex parte Johnson* (CO/1467/94) "any reasonable bench of Justices must have realised, the means inquiry required by Regulation 41(2) is of great importance because without it the Justices plainly cannot properly arrive at a conclusion as to whether the failure to pay had been due to the debtor's wilful refusal or culpable neglect. A means inquiry, thus, is at the centre of the enforcement procedure which is laid down by these Regulations. The[se] Justices did not, in truth, embark upon a proper means inquiry at all. It follows that their order committing the applicant to prison is entirely vitiated."
(ii) the decision of the Justices to commit the applicant to a period of imprisonment of 28 days in respect of Community Charge arrears of £228.63 placing the applicant in an inferior position to a person convicted of a criminal offence and being subject to the limitations of Schedule 4 of the Magistrates Court Act 1980 was unreasonable.
(iii) the decision of the Justices to commit the applicant to an immediate term of imprisonment in her absence was unlawful in that they could not have been satisfied that the applicant had received proper notice of the hearing see Mr. Justice Jowitt in *R v. Hyndburn Justices ex parte Woolag[h]an* [unreported 2nd December 1995]: "The difficulty, though, for the Magistrates is, that when there is no appearance before them, they really have no way of telling whether this may be one of those, no doubt not over frequent cases in which a letter has miscarried for one reason or another, perhaps because it has not been delivered or because the charge payer is absent for a continuing period from home, or because, in premises with a number of separate occupiers, a letter has got into the wrong hands. It seems therefore, to follow that where there has been service by ordinary post, careful consideration would have to be given to the particular circumstances of the charge payer, before, if ever, concluding that the notice must have come into his hands ... there being no proof of service ... the applicant is entitled to succeed and the Order of Certiorari must go to quash the committal warrant"
(iv) in view of the applicant's circumstances, the time that has elapsed since the applicant was imprisoned and the period of time spent in prison, all parties agree that this matter be not remitted to the Magistrates."

May PARKER 46416/99 Days in prison Two After 1st June 1997
Grounds why order quashed:
udgment of Mr. Justice Laws of 15 December 1998
"The case in a nutshell may be described thus. The Scunthorpe Magistrates issued a warrant of commitment against this applicant, in circumstances where outstanding community charge in the sum of £11.47 had already been paid, although after the issue of the liability order; and all that was outstanding at the time of the warrant's issue was £40 costs.
It is clear from regulation 41 subregulation 2, 3 and 46 (4) of the Community Charge Administration Enforcement Regulations 1989 that the magistrates lacked all power to issue a warrant of commitment in those circumstances. Accordingly I quash the warrant."

Debra MACKMAN 47143/99 Days in prison Five Both Before 1st June 1997
Grounds why order quashed:

"(i) The decision of the Justices that the applicant had culpably neglected to pay her Community Charge without having conducted an enquiry into her circumstances as of the time that the liability became due was unlawful, see *R v. Leeds Justices ex parte Kennett* [1996] RVR 53.

(ii) The decision of the Justices to issue a sentence of committal to prison and to make an order postponing the issue of the warrant that would have left the threat of imprisonment over her for over 5 years was unlawful having regard to the principles laid down in *R v. Oliver and Oliver* [1989] 11 Cr App R(S) 10 and *R v. Ealing Justices ex parte Cloves* [1991] RVR 169 and *R v. Newcastle upon Tyne Justices ex parte Devine* [1988] RA 97."

Mandy MASON 47144/99 Days in prison Three After 1st June 1997
Grounds why order quashed:

"(i) The decision of the Justices to make a finding that the applicant had culpably neglected to pay [her] fines was unreasonable, "to be open to criticism for the disposal of slender resources is one thing; to be found guilty of culpable neglect in the disposal of them is another" see *R v. South Tyneside Justices ex parte Martin* CO/1755/94 and *R v Woking Justices ex parte Johnstone* [1942] 2 All ER 179. The Justices must be satisfied beyond reasonable doubt of the applicant's wilful refusal or culpable neglect before making such a finding. On the evidence before them, the Justices could not properly have made a finding that she did not have good reason for failing to discharge her liability to the required standard of proof, see *R v Erewash Borough Council and Ilkeston Justices ex parte Smedburg and Smedburg* [1993] RVR 34, *R v Mid Herts Justices ex parte Cox* [1995] JP 507.

(ii) The decision of the Justices to issue a sentence of committal to prison and to make an order postponing the issue of the warrant that would have left the threat of imprisonment over the applicant for in excess of 4 and a half years was unlawful having regard to the principles laid down in *R v Oliver and Oliver* [1989] 11 Cr App R(S) 10, *R v Ealing Justices ex parte Cloves* [1991] RVR 169 and *R v Newcastle Justices ex parte Devine* [1998] TLR 23.4.98.

(iii) The decision of the Justices to issue a warrant committing the applicant to a period of 50 days imprisonment in [her] absence was unlawful without having evidence that [she] received proper notice of the hearing before them, see Lord Justice Rose in *R v Doncaster Justices ex parte Hannan* CO/1424/98 "This case illustrates how unwise it may be for Justices to make an order committing someone to prison when they do not know, because that person is not before them and because that person does not know of the date of the hearing, what the [up to] date circumstances are. It seems to me that, knowing that the applicant had not been served with notice of the proceedings, the Justices ought, much more prudently, to have adjourned the question of whether or not the warrant of commitment should be issued until such later time as she had been served with notice of the proceedings. For my part, I am satisfied that, in issuing the warrant in the circumstances in which they did, the Justices did act perversely and ... I would quash the order which they made".

(iv) In view of the circumstances of the applicant and [her] detention, and the period of detention served, all parties agree that the matter be remitted back to the Magistrates and that the Magistrates upon reviewing the matter agree to remit the outstanding fines, see Brooke LJ in *R v St Helens Justices ex parte Jones* CO/3328/95."

Mark WOOD 47441/99 Days in prison Five Before 1st June 1997
Grounds why order quashed:

"(a) The Justices erred in law on 28th February 1996 in that they:
(i) failed to conduct inquiries into each period leading to the granting of each liability order as required by Regulation 41(2) of the Community Charges (Administration and Enforcement) Regulations 1989, see *R v. Leeds Justices ex parte Kennett* [1996] RVR 53,
(ii) could not have been properly satisfied on the evidence before them that the Applicant had culpably neglected to have paid the sums due,
(iii) failed to give proper consideration to the possibility of deducting the Applicant's lia bility from his income support, see *R v. Alfreton Justices ex parte Gratton*, The Times, 7 December 1993, and
(iv) were unreasonable to have fixed a disproportionate sentence.
(b) The Justices erred in law on 10 March 1997 in that they:
(i) failed to satisfy themselves that the conditions precedent to the issue of committal warrants had been satisfied[2],
(ii) failed to ensure that the Applicant was given the opportunity to be represented, and
(iii) issued warrants for a period of imprisonment in excess of the period announced in open court."

Christine HOUGHTON 47985/99 Days in prison Three After 1st June 1997
Grounds why order quashed:

"(i) The decision of the Justices to issue the warrant committing the applicant to prison in her absence and not to adjourn the proceedings in order to enable the applicant to attend before the Justices was unreasonable having regard to the evidence of her incapacity.
(ii) In view of the circumstances of the applicant and her detention, and the period of detention served, all parties agree that the matter be remitted back to the Magistrates and that the Magistrates reduce the term of imprisonment ordered on the 1st October 1998 to 3 days, being the period of imprisonment served, see *R v Mid Herts Justices ex parte Cox* [1995] JP 507."

[2] In the Affidavit of the applicant's solicitor that accompanied his application for judicial review in the High Court it is stated that, according to both the applicant and the representative of the charging authority who was present in court on 10 March 1997, the magistrates did not make any finding of culpable neglect or wilful refusal before committing the applicant to prison

Tracey WATTS 53062/99 Days in prison Two Both Before 1st June 1997

Grounds why order quashed:

"(i) In the light of the subsequent case-law the decision of the Justices of the 20th October 1997 to issue a warrant committing the applicant to a period of 7 days imprisonment in her absence was unlawful without having evidence that [she] received proper notice of the hearing before them, see Lord Justice Rose in *R v Doncaster Justices ex parte Hannan* CO/1424/98 and *R v Doncaster Justices ex parte Christison*

and *R v Doncaster Justices ex parte Jack* [TLR 25th May 1999] "The time had come to make it clear to justices that in the view of the court it was difficult to concede that there would be circumstances to justify the making of the committal order when the defendant failed to appear before the court. The justices would be unable to ascertain the reason why payment was not made and whether that could be excused. The circumstances of the defendant may have changed such that it might be wrong to commit. Committal was a last resort to extract payment. Justices had a sensible, powerful weapon in the form of a warrant not backed for bail, and that was the means by which a person brought to court could be made to explain why she had not paid. Justices would then have the information to decide whether to commit. His Lordship could not emphasise strongly enough that there needed to be exceptional circumstances, and his Lordship was bound to say that it was difficult to see where there would be such circumstances, in which to commit to prison."

(ii) In view of the circumstances of the applicant and her detention, and the period of detention served, all parties agree that the matter be remitted back to the magistrates and that the magistrates, upon reviewing the matter agree to remit the outstanding fines, see Brooke LJ in *R. v. St. Helens Justices ex parte Jones*."

Martin SLATER 2460/03 Days in prison Five Both Before 1st June 1997

Grounds why order quashed:

The applicant was under 21 years of age at the time of his hearings before the magistrates.

"That it is arguable that in ordering that the Applicant be committed to prison for 28 days without making any express reference to the possibility of deduction from income support, the Metropolitan Stipendiary Magistrate acted unreasonably."

Kathleen PITT 53111/99 Days in prison Four Both Before 1st June 1997

Grounds why order quashed:

"(i) The Justices were UNLAWFUL in committing the Applicant to prison in that they failed to have proper regard to the purpose of imprisonment and the alternatives available and that they failed to endorse the warrant of commitment accordingly, see Simon Brown LJ in *Re: Cawley and Others* [1996] 160 JP 133 "... It must be possible to see from the [face] of the warrant (and register) why it is that, very exceptionally one hopes, the Justices have felt no alternative but to commit this young person to custody" in particular as to why the alternatives of the issue of a warrant for her attendance before the court, a Fines Supervision Order or deductions from Income Support would have been inappropriate or unsuccessful, see also *R v Exeter City Justices ex parte Sugar* [1992] 157 JP 766, *R v Havering Magistrates Court ex parte Molloy* [1994] COD 187 and Farquharson J in *R v Norwich Magistrates Court ex parte Lilly* [1987] 151 JP 689, "to go through the judicial exercise of seeing if there was any other method of enforcing payment of the fine, short of committing the applicant to prison, and that necessarily included a procedure whereby [he] was examined as to what property or other earnings or income [he] might have. It is not [to be assumed] merely on their experience of other cases by the justices that the proceeding is a formality or unnecessary".

(ii) In view of the circumstances of the applicant, and the period of detention served, the matter be not remitted back to the Magistrates."

Patricia FLETCHER 2482/03 Days in prison Three Both Before 1st June 1997
Grounds why order quashed:

"(i) The Justices were UNLAWFUL in committing the Applicant to prison in that they failed to have proper regard to the purpose of imprisonment and the alternatives available including the establishment of a Fines Supervision Order or deductions from Income Support, in such cases see *Re Cawley* [1996] 160 JP 133, *R v Exeter City Justices ex parte Sugar* [1992] 157 JP 766, *R v Havering Magistrates Court ex parte Molloy* [1994] COD 187 and Farquharson J in *R v Norwich Magistrates Court ex parte Lilly* [1987] 151 JP 689, "to go through the judicial exercise of seeing if there was any other method of enforcing payment of the fine, short of committing the applicant to prison, and that necessarily included a procedure whereby [he] was examined as to what property or other earnings or income [he] might have. It is not [to be assumed] merely on their experience of other cases by the justices that the proceeding is a formality or unnecessary". The applicant gave evidence that she was in receipt of £83.74 per week Income Support and that she had deductions of £14.46 in respect of the recovery of a social fund loan. Regulation 4 of the Fines (Deductions from Income Support) Regulations 1992 stipulates the circumstances in which, upon application from the Clerk to the Justices, the Secretary of State shall make deductions from Income Support. Regulation 4(1)(a) stipulates that no deduction shall be made where the deduction would result in an aggregate deduction of items listed in Regulation 4(1)(b)(i) to (vii) exceeds £7.20 per week. Regulation 4(2)(a) stipulates that no deduction shall be made if such a reduction would result in an award on Income Support of less than 10 pence per week. As there was no evidence before the Justices that the applicant was having deductions for any of the items listed in Regulation 4(1)(b)(i) to (vii) or that, as a result of a deduction for the recovery of fines, her Income Support entitlement would fall below 10 pence per week, there was no impediment on the recovery of fines by deductions from Income Support.
(ii) In view of the circumstances of the applicant, and the period of detention served, the matter be not remitted back to the Magistrates."

Mary MIDDLETON 2483/03 Days in prison Two Both Before 1st June 1997
Grounds why order quashed:

"(i) The Justices were UNLAWFUL in committing the applicant to an immediate term of imprisonment without having regard to the provisions of Section 82 and 84 of the Magistrates Courts Act, see Simon Brown LJ in *Re: Cawley and Others* (CO/1832/95), 28th November 1995 transcript at page 28 "... It must be possible to see from the [face] of the warrant (and register) why it is that, very exceptionally one hopes, the Justices have felt no alternative but to commit this young person to custody" in particular as to why the alternatives of a Fines Supervision Order or the passing of a term of imprisonment but suspending the issue of the warrant on terms would have been inappropriate or unsuccessful.

(ii) The Justices were unreasonable in committing the applicant to an immediate term of imprisonment in that they failed to have proper regard to the purpose of imprisonment in such cases, see *R v. Alfreton Justices ex parte Gratton* CO/484/93, transcript at page 4 per Mr Justice Macpherson of Cluny, "...we all know now as a result of a number of decisions that community charge liability should only be visited with prison ... if there is no other way in which the money can be extracted. Prison is not to be used as a big stick or primarily as punishment but as a means of extracting the liability" and Farquharson J in *R v. Norwich Magistrates Court ex parte Lilly* [1987] 151 JP 689 "to go through the judicial exercise of seeing if there was any other method of enforcing payment of the fine, short of committing the applicant to prison, and that necessarily included a procedure whereby [he] was examined as to what property or other earnings or income [he] might have. It is not [to be assumed] merely on their experience of other cases by the justices that the proceeding is a formality or unnecessary".

(iii) **in view of the circumstances of this application and the period of time spent in prison the matter be not remitted back to the Magistrates."**

Lisa SHELLEY 2484/03 Days in prison Two Both Before 1st June 1997
Grounds why order quashed:

"(i) The Justices were UNLAWFUL in committing the applicant to prison in that they failed to have proper regard to the purpose of imprisonment and the alternatives available and that they failed to endorse the warrant of commitment accordingly, see Simon Brown LJ in *Re: Cawley and Others* [1996] 160 JP 133 "... It must be possible to see from the [face] of the warrant (and register) why it is that, very exceptionally one hopes, the Justices have felt no alternative but to commit this young person to custody" in particular as to why the alternatives of the issue of a warrant for her attendance before the court, a Fines Supervision Order or deductions from Income Support would have been inappropriate or unsuccessful, see also *R v. Exeter City Justices ex parte Sugar* [1992] 157 JP 766, *R v. Havering Magistrates Court ex parte Molloy* [1994] COD 187 and Farquharson J in *R v. Norwich Magistrates Court ex parte Lilly* [1987] 151 JP 689, "to go through the judicial exercise of seeing if there was any other method of enforcing payment of the fine, short of committing the applicant to prison, and that necessarily included a procedure whereby [he] was examined as to what property or other earnings or income [he] might have. It is not [to be assumed] merely on their experience of other cases by the justices that the proceeding is a formality or unnecessary"

(ii) in view of the circumstances of the applicant, and the period of detention served, the matter be not remitted back to the Magistrates"

Suzanne JELLEY 54969/00 Days in prison Four Before 1st June 1997
Grounds why order quashed:

"(i) The Justices are unable to evidence from the face of the warrant or the records available at the court office the procedural steps followed in committing the Applicant to prison in default of paying the particular financial penalties. Since the decision complained of dates back to 8th December 1994 the passage of time makes it difficult for the Justices and their Clerk to recall events and therefore impossible for them to file affidavit evidence. In the light of recent case-law, *Re: Cawley and Others* [1996] 160 JP 133 it is conceded that the High Court cannot but find in the Applicant's favour.

(ii) In view of the circumstances of the applicant, and the period of detention served, the matter be not remitted back to the Magistrates."

Anita MERRY 54973/00 Days in prison Two 1st June 1997
Grounds why order quashed:

"The decision of the Justices on the 22nd December 1994 to issue terms of imprisonment that would have 'hung over' the applicant for nearly 4 years was unreasonable, see *R v. Newcastle Justices ex parte Devine, R v. Oliver & Oliver* and *R v. Stockport Justices ex parte Conlon"*

Beverley WATSON 54997/00 Days in prison Two Before 1st June 1997
Grounds why order quashed:

The applicant was under 21 years of age at the time of her hearings before the magistrates.

"(i) The Justices were UNLAWFUL in committing the Applicant to prison in that they failed to have proper regard to the purpose of imprisonment and the alternatives available including the establishment of a Fines Supervision Order or deductions from Income Support, in such cases *R v. Exeter City Justices ex parte Sugar* [1992] 157 JP 766, *R v. Havering Magistrates Court ex parte Molloy* [1994] COD 187 and Farquharson J in *R v. Norwich Magistrates Court ex parte Lilly* [1987] 151 JP 689, "to go through the judicial exercise of seeing if there was any other method of enforcing payment of the fine, short of committing the applicant to prison, and that necessarily included a procedure whereby [he] was examined as to what property or other earnings or income [he] might have. It is not [to be assumed] merely on their experience of other cases by the justices that the proceeding is a formality or unnecessary"

(ii) The Justices were UNLAWFUL in committing the Applicant to prison in that they failed to have proper regard to the procedure for the committal to prison of under 21 year olds in respect of fines default and that they failed to endorse the warrant of commitment accordingly, see Simon Brown LJ in *Re: Cawley and Others* [1996] 160 JP 133 "... it must be possible to see from the [face] of the warrant (register) why it is that, very exceptionally one hopes, the Justices have felt no alternative but to commit this young person to custody" in particular as to why the alternatives of the issue of a warrant for her attendance before the court, a Fines Supervision Order or deductions from Income Support would have been inappropriate or unsuccessful.

(iii) In view of the circumstances of the applicant, and the period of detention served the matter be not remitted back to the Magistrates."

Jean JACKSON 55068/00 Days in prison Two Before 1st June 1997
Grounds why order quashed:

"In the light of the subsequent case-law, the decision of the Justices of the 7th October 1993 to issue a warrant committing the applicant to a period of 7 days imprisonment in her absence was unlawful without having evidence that [she] received proper notice of the hearing before them, see Lord Justice Rose in *R v. Doncaster Justices ex parte Hannan* CO/1424/98 and *R v. Doncaster Justices ex parte Christison* and *R v. Doncaster Justices ex parte Jack* [TLR 25th May 1999] 'The time had come to make it clear to Justices that in the view of the court it was difficult to concede that there would be circumstances to justify the making of the committal order when the defendant failed to appear before the court. The Justices would be unable to ascertain the reason why payment was not made and whether that could be excused. The circumstances of the defendant may have changed such that it might be wrong to commit. Committal was a last resort to extract payment. Justices had a sensible, powerful weapon in the form of a warrant not backed for bail, and that was the means by which a person brought to court could be made to explain why she had not paid. Justices would then have the information to decide whether to commit. His Lordship could not emphasise strongly enough that there needed to be exceptional circumstances, and his Lordship was bound to say that it was difficult to see where there would be such circumstances, in which to commit to prison."

Jason TAYLOR 56231/00 Days in prison Two After 1st June 1997

Grounds why order quashed:

The applicant was under 21 years of age at the time of his hearings before the magistrates.

"(i) The decision of the Justices to proceed to hear an application for the applicant's committal to prison without giving him the opportunity to secure appropriate representation was unlawful, see Section 3 of the Criminal Justice Act 1982 *Re: McC (A Minor)* [1985] 1 AC 528.

The decision of the Justices to make a finding that the applicant had wilfully refused or culpably neglected to pay his fines without conducting adequate enquiry into his means and circumstances was unlawful, see *R v. Stafford Justices ex parte Johnson* CO/1476/94.

The decision of the Justices that the applicant had further wilfully refused, culpably neglected or did not have good reason for his failure to pay his fines as ordered was unreasonable.

The failure of the Justices to announce their reasons for rejecting the alternatives to imprisonment prior to issuing the warrant of commitment was unlawful."

Elizabeth DONALD 56109/00 Days in prison Two Before 1st June 1997

Grounds why order quashed:

"The decision of the Justices [to] proceed to consider the application for [her] committal to prison and to issue warrants for [her] committal to prison in [her] absence without having evidence as to the effective service of the notice of the hearing was unlawful, see Lord Justice Rose in *R v. Doncaster Justices ex parte Hannan* CO/1424/98 'This case illustrates how unwise it may be for Justices to make an order committing someone to prison when they do not know, because that person is not before them and because that person does not know of the date of the hearing, what the [up to] date circumstances are. It seems to me that, knowing that the applicant had not been served with notice of the proceedings, the Justices ought, much more prudently, to have adjourned the question of whether or not the warrant of commitment should be issued until such later time as she had been served with notice of the proceedings. For my part, I am satisfied that, in issuing the warrant in the circumstances in which they did the Justices did act perversely and ... I would quash the order which they made' and see Mr Justice Collins in *R v. Doncaster Justices ex parte Christison* and *R v. Doncaster Justices ex parte Jack* [TLR 25th May 1999] 'The time had come to make it clear to Justices that in the view of the court it was difficult to concede that there would be circumstances to justify the making of the committal order when the defendant failed to appear before the court. The Justices would be unable to ascertain the reason why payment was not made and whether that could be excused. The circumstances of the defendant may have changed such that it might be wrong to commit. Committal was a last resort to extract payment. Justices had a sensible, powerful weapon in the form of a warrant not backed for bail, and that was the means by which a person brought to court could be made to explain why she had not paid. Justices would then have the information to decide whether to commit. His Lordship could not emphasise strongly enough that there needed to be exceptional circumstances, and his Lordship was bound to say that it was difficult to see where there would be such circumstances, in which to commit to prison."

Leanne ARMSTRONG 55046/00 Days in prison Two Before 1st June 1997

Grounds why order quashed:

"The Justices were UNREASONABLE in committing the Applicant to prison in that they failed to have proper regard to the purpose of imprisonment and the alternatives available including the establishment of a Fines Supervision Order or deductions from Income Support, in such cases see *R v. Exeter City Justices ex parte Sugar* [1992] 157 JP 766, *R v. Havering Magistrates Court ex parte Molloy* [1994] COD 187 and Farquharson J in *R v. Norwich Magistrates Court ex parte Lilly* [1987] 151 JP 689, 'to go through the judicial exercise of seeing if there was any other method of enforcing payment of the fine, short of committing the applicant to prison, and that necessarily included a procedure whereby [he] was examined as to what property or other earnings or income [he] might have. It is not [to be assumed] merely on their experience of other cases by the justices that the proceeding is a formality or unnecessary'"

Geraldine TAYLOR 55071/00 Days in prison Three Before 1st June 1997

Grounds why order quashed:

"(i) The Justices were UNLAWFUL in issuing a warrant committing the applicant to prison without fully fulfilling the requirements of Section 88 of the Magistrates Court Act 1980.

The Justices were UNREASONABLE in committing the applicant to prison in that they failed to have proper regard to the purpose of imprisonment and the alternatives available including issue of a warrant for her attendance before the Court or the establishment of a Fines Supervision Order or deductions from Income Support, see *R v. Alfreton Justices ex parte Gratton* CO/484/93, transcript at page 4 per Mr Justice Macpherson of Cluny, '...We all know now as the result of a number of decisions that community charge liability should only be visited with prison ... if there is no other way in which the money can be extracted. Prison is not to be used as a big stick or primarily as a punishment but as a means of extracting the liability' and Farquharson J in *R v. Norwich Magistrates Court ex parte Lilly* [1987] 151 JP 689, "to go through the judicial exercise of seeing if there was any other method of enforcing payment of the fine, short of committing the applicant to prison, and that necessarily included a procedure whereby [he] was examined as to what property or other earnings or income [he] might have. It is not [to be assumed] merely on their experience of other cases by the justices that the proceeding is a formality or unnecessary".

In view of the circumstances of the applicant and the period of detention served, the matter be not remitted back to the Magistrates."

Rachel CONDON 56233/00 Days in prison Three Both 1st June 1997

Grounds why order quashed:

"The Justices were unreasonable in committing the Applicant to an immediate term of imprisonment in that they failed to have proper regard to the purpose of imprisonment in the light of the fact that she was in receipt of Income Support, thereby giving the Justices the opportunity to recover the outstanding fine by way of deductions from Income Support, the welfare of the applicant and her child. The Justices failed to have due regard to the purpose of the Fines Enforcement legislation being to coerce payment which could have been secured by virtue of an order that fines arrears be recovered under the Fines (Deductions from Income Support) Regulations 1992 and not to punish, the punishment being the fine itself, see Farquharson J in *R. v. Norwich Magistrates Court ex parte Lilly* [1987] 151 JP 689, 'to go through the judicial exercise of seeing if there was any other method of enforcing payment of the fine, short of committing the applicant to prison, and that necessarily included a procedure whereby [he] was examined as to what property or other earnings or income [he] might have. It is not [to be assumed] merely on their experience of other cases by the justices that the proceeding is a formality or unnecessary'"

Allison CHRISTISON 56429/00 Days in prison Two After 1st June 1997
Grounds why order quashed:
Judgment of Mr Justice Collins of 13 May 1999
(See under the heading "The circumstances of the cases" above)

Lisa REILLY 56232/00 Days in prison One Both 1st June 1997
Grounds why order quashed:

"(i) The decision of the Justices on the 28th November 1996 that the applicant had culpably neglected to pay her Community Charge and Council Tax was unreasonable, see *Meara v. DPP* (CO/2983/98), *R v. Manchester Justices ex parte Davies* 152 JP 221, 'to be open to criticism for the disposal of slender resources is one thing; to be found guilty of culpable neglect in the disposal of them is another', *R v. South Tyneside Justices ex parte Martin* CO 1755/95 and *R v. Woking Justices ex parte Johnstone* [1942] 2 All ER 179

The decisions of the Justices on the 12th March 1998 and 21st March 1998 to issue warrants committing the applicant to a period of 28 days' imprisonment in her absence without having evidence that she had received proper notice of the hearing before them was unlawful, see Mr Justice Collins in *R v. Doncaster Justices ex parte Christison* and

R v. Doncaster Justices ex parte Jack [TLR 25th May 1999] "The time had come to make it clear to Justices that in the view of the court it was difficult to concede that there would be circumstances to justify the making of the committal order when the defendant failed to appear before the court. The Justices would be unable to ascertain the reason why payment was not made and whether that could be excused. The circumstances of the defendant may have changed such that it might be wrong to commit. Committal was a last resort to extract payment. Justices had a sensible, powerful weapon in the form of a warrant not backed for bail, and that was the means by which a person brought to court could be made to explain why she had not paid. Justices would then have the information to decide whether to commit. His Lordship could not emphasise strongly enough that there needed to be exceptional circumstances, and his Lordship was bound to say that it was difficult to see where there would be such circumstances, in which to commit to prison."
In view of the acute personal circumstances of the applicant and her detention, and the period of detention served, all parties agree that the matter be remitted back to the Magistrates, see Brooke LJ in *R v. St Helens Justices ex parte Jones*."

Gillian WILSON 56441/00 Days in prison Two After 1st June 1997
Grounds why order quashed:
"(i) The decision of the Justices to issue a warrant committing the applicant to a period of 7 days imprisonment in her absence was unlawful without having evidence that she had received proper notice of the hearing before them, see Lord Justice Rose in *R v. Doncaster Justices ex parte Hannan* CO/1424/98 'This case illustrates how unwise it may be for Justices to make an order committing someone to prison when they do not know, because that person is not before them, and because that person does not know of the date of the hearing, what the up to date circumstances are. It seems to me that, knowing that the Applicant had not been served with notice of proceedings, the Justices ought, much more prudently, to have adjourned the question of whether or not the warrant of commitment should be issued until such later time as she had been served with notice of the proceedings. For my part, I am satisfied that, in issuing the warrant in the circumstances in which they did, the Justices did act perversely and ... I would quash the order which they made'.
(ii) In view of the circumstances of the Applicant and her detention, and the period of detention served, all parties agree that the matter be remitted back to the Magistrates and that the Magistrates upon reviewing the matter agree to remit the outstanding fines, see Brooke LJ in *R v. St Helens Justice ex parte Jones* CO/3328/95."

A GUIDE TO THE MAGISTRATES' COURTS (AMENDMENT) RULES 2019 (S.I. 2019/1367)

Where to find the new Rules
The Magistrates' Courts (Amendment) Rules 2019 are at this address:

http://www.legislation.gov.uk/uksi/2019/1367/pdfs/uksi_20191367_en.pdf

When the Rules come into force, the changes they make will appear at this address, too:

https://www.justice.gov.uk/courts/procedure-rules/other-procedure-rules-for-magistratescourts-and-the-crown-court

What the new Rules are for The new Rules amend the Magistrates' Courts Rules 1981. These rules govern civil proceedings in magistrates' courts. They:

• Remove the requirement for signatures on summonses and warrants .

• Prescribe the form of warrants of arrest.

• Prescribe the form of summonses.

• Amend the rules on service of summonses to permit modern methods of communication such as email or cloud access.

• Introduce a new rule on service of orders, other than liability orders.

• Specify the time at which service of summonses and orders is deemed to take place.

When the new rules come into force.

The rules come into force on Wednesday 1 st January 2020.

What is in the new Rules Removing the requirement for signatures on summonses, warrants, and other orders.

A summons is the usual method of commencing a civil case in magistrates' courts, although other methods apply in some types of proceedings. Summonses are also used in criminal proceedings in magistrates' courts, although other methods, such as arrest and charge, or requisition, are available to public prosecutors. A person bringing civil proceedings (a 'complainant') makes a formal 'complaint' to the court, asking the court to issue a summons. The summons is usually prepared and served by the complainant. Traditionally all summonses were signed with the name of the judge, magistrate or justices' legal adviser issuing them, but this requirement was removed in 2010 in criminal proceedings.
Rule 7 dispenses with the requirement for a signature provided the court office keeps a record of issue. Complainants will no longer need to affix the name of the issuing officer on the summons.

Warrants are court orders requiring a third party to compel a person to go either to court or to prison. Rule 5 dispenses with the requirement that warrants are signed, subject to any statutory requirement for a signature. Again, there must be a record of the person issuing the warrant.

Finally, rule 9 removes rule 109 of the Magistrates' Courts Rules, which set out rules for signatures on prescribed court forms, particularly allowing them to be signed by a court officer. Rule 109 was already of limited effect, since most court forms were deprescribed in 2001 and all but four of the remainder ceased to be of effect following the adoption of the Criminal Procedure Rules. The four remaining comprise three forms of complaint, which are 2 only necessary if the court issues a 'first instance' warrant, and a stated case. The effect is to require these documents to be signed by the justices. However, it is settled law that signatures can be made other than in wet ink, for example electronically or by a stamp.

Prescribing the form of summonses

Rule 7 also changes the requirements for summonses.

The rule specifying that a summons can contain more than one complaint has been simplified.

Some obvious formalities have been specified for the first time, for example that the name of the complainant appears on the summons. Others have been preserved from the previous form of the Rule, for example the requirement to include the date and place of the hearing.

For the first time, a summons must include the name and address of the court office dealing with the case. This ensures that defendants can contact the court if necessary, even if the office is not in the same building as the courthouse.

Prescribing the form of warrants of arrest

Rule 5 makes similar changes are made to the form of warrants, in addition requiring them to show the name of the person to be detained and the name of the person assigned to execute the warrant. This expands and replaces Rule 96(2) which Rule 6 removes.

Amending the rules on service of summonses

The Rules before amendment required summonses to be served only by post, or by handing to the defendant, or leaving at their last known address. This lags far behind the Criminal Procedure Rules and the Civil Procedure Rules which apply in other civil courts, which allow methods of communication developed since 1981. Rule 8 expands the methods of service to add service by email, document repository, document exchange, service on a legal representative and, where the defendant is in prison, on the governor. In addition, where all these methods are unsuitable or unsuccessful, the court can specify other means of service, for example by text message or through a third party.

Rule 8 also sets out the time in which a summons will be deemed to have been served by each method.

Finally, Rule 8 sets out exceptions to the rules on service in relation to witness summonses and judgement summonses.

A new rule on service of orders

Rule 10 inserts a new Rule specifying that the court officer must serve a court order and setting out the methods of service. There was previously no provision in the Rules for service of orders. In the main, the method of service is prescribed in the legislation creating the order. That means that this Rule will only apply where service is not already prescribed. It is hoped that where new orders are created, they will use this provision, removing the need for a further set of rules on service.

The Rule does not apply to liability orders, for example in council tax enforcement. Complainants will continue to notify defendants in these cases.

Legal Operations,
HM Courts Service
23 October 2019

Conclusion

I'm hoping that this book will help people lose the fear of getting into council tax arrears and fearing the knock at the door by the enforcement agents.

In 2024/25 95% of councils are going to raise council tax up to the maximum increase 4.99%

Birmingham, Woking, Slough and Thurrock have special dispensation to raise council tax by 10%

We are told councils are having to make some of their toughest decisions ever to prevent the risk of insolvency over £9bn funding black hole over the next five years.

These decisions are not having to be made from lack of money, it's down to mismanaged funds.

Many residents are already suffering with thousands of pounds of council tax arrears, many suffering with the threats of removal of their goods, and only in England the threats of imprisonment for non payment of a local tax which is a civil matter.

It seems that the local authorities and Government don't seem to realise or even care that further raises in council tax will just create more non payers, more people suffering with depression, metal health issues and abuse.

Most are not refusing to pay, but can't pay, but councils treat them all mostly the same. The financial branch of the local authorities are very unpleasant people to deal with.

There is massive harassment and bullying by the local authorities financial department against the residents who fall in to arrears.

There is no such thing as morality or ethics in the collection of council tax. The behaviour of the local authorities has been disgraceful in the courts. Councils get privilege in the way matters are heard in magistrates court.

This bad behaviour is also seen in the enforcement agents the councils employ to go out and harass mainly the poorest in our society. Most these enforcement agents only get their wage on collection of a debt. These agents can not force entry, they can only enter through open or unlocked doors.

'All of the funding raised through council tax can be spent as the local authority sees fit. It is not possible to say that council tax pays for particular local services: it is pooled with revenue from business rates, Government grants and other sources of income.

In law council tax is a tax, **not a fee or charge for local authority public services.** There is no entitlement to a refund of council tax if a constituent believes that a particular local service has not been provided.

Printed in Great Britain
by Amazon

57639573R00090